ENCOUNTERING JESUS
A Holy Land Experience

VINCENZO PERONI
·······

FOREWORD BY GREG FRIEDMAN, OFM

PREFACE BY ARCHBISHOP PIERBATTISTA PIZZABALLA, OFM

WATERCOLOR SKETCHES BY ALESSANDRO ALGHISI

ENGLISH TRANSLATION BY MARSHA DAIGLE-WILLIAMSON

franciscan
media®
Cincinnati, Ohio

Cover and book design by Mark Sullivan
Cover image by Alessandro Alghisi

Library of Congress Control Number: 2020930868

ISBN 978-1-63253-315-9

Published by Franciscan Media
28 W. Liberty St.
Cincinnati, OH 45202
www.FranciscanMedia.org

To those who dwell in, maintain, and love the Holy Land

· · · · · · ·

Sincere thanks to friends who encouraged this publication and in particular to Simonetta Tinelli for collecting the recordings and transcribing their texts and to Filly Balice for editing them.

CONTENTS

· · · · · · ·

FOREWORD

· · · · · · ·

The book you are holding is a work of faith, love, and friendship. It originated with the faith of its author. Monsignor Vincenzo Peroni's love for the Holy Land prompted him to write the beautiful reflections contained in these pages. His friendship with the Franciscans of the Holy Land has helped to make possible its publication for an English-speaking audience. I was honored to be the channel to pass the book along to Fr. Dan Kroger at Franciscan Media, where it found a home. When I first read over the reflections contained here, I knew that it would be a wonderful companion for Holy Land pilgrims—whether they actually travel there or visit as "armchair pilgrims" from home.

As a guide for pilgrims in the Holy Land and in Italy, I rely on a simple model which was shared with me by my fellow Franciscans when I first went on pilgrimage to the places where Saints Francis and Clare of Assisi lived. That model can be expressed simply as: PLACE-EVENT-SPIRITUALITY.

Place: A pilgrim travels to a holy place. I tell my pilgrims—and indeed anyone on a faith-journey—that a "holy" place may be defined in many ways. Of course, the places you will visit in this book are truly the "Holy Land" for those who believe in Jesus. (They are holy to Jews and Muslims, for a variety of reasons as well.) The presence of Our Lord; Mary, his Mother; the disciples, and countless Christians down through the ages helps us to call these places "holy."

But other places may be holy to you or me! Your parish church, your family home, a favorite place in nature—any of these and more can be "holy" because of how you have met God there. This realization makes pilgrimage possible anywhere, for anyone!

Event: At a holy place, a pilgrim tells the story. When I guide Holy Land pilgrims to a shrine, I read the Gospel account which pertains to that place. In fact, in determining "how authentic" a place is (a question asked on every Holy Land pilgrimage!) an important criterion is the fact that pilgrims over the centuries sought out possible locations for most Gospel stories. Not every Holy Land shrine is "100 percent authentic." What matters is being able to tell the story here—where God chose to be born as a human being, to grow up, to minister, and to suffer, die and rise.

This search is a very human way to express our belief in the Incarnation: The Word became flesh in a particular time and place! As Christians, we want to enter as much as possible into that reality. We may not know exactly where Jesus preached, but when we stand on the shore of the Sea of Galilee, the hills, the water, the wind—all bring home to us what his first disciples experienced.

Your own stories of faith—the ones you tell in the place where you grew up, the church where you were baptized, the mountains you hike in as an adult—bring home to you how God has graced your life.

Spirituality: The pilgrim is open to what God wants to do in his or her life. As a guide, I can take pilgrims to the place. I can tell the story. But then we must turn things over to God. Sometimes, the experience of God moving in one's life might come months, even years later. One couple shared with me how the Scriptures at daily Mass meant so much more to them after their return home from pilgrimage.

That has been my experience again and again—as I pray the Psalms each day and allow the Holy Spirit to connect the imagery of desert and mountain to come to mind and reinforce how the story of salvation is rooted there, in the Holy Land.

Monsignor Peroni, in the reflections contained in this book, is concerned primarily with the second and third steps in the "pilgrimage model." He envisions that the reader is at least somewhat familiar with the places treated here. And that first step— "place"—is something even an "armchair pilgrim" can take, thanks to images available in print and online. The sensitive illustrations by Alessandro Alghisi in this book can help. In any case, it is less important that the reader be standing on the shore of the Sea of Galilee, than to imagine the place, and move quickly to the "event."

Thanks to the author, each chapter contains Scripture texts which set the scene. These can be read slowly and reflectively, allowing the original storytellers, the evangelists, to be your "pilgrim guide."

It is with the third step of pilgrimage—"spirituality"—that Monsignor Peroni has created a most valuable resource. He has written beautiful reflections, probing questions, and sensitive prayers to gently take you from the story to the place where you can allow God—in silence—to touch your life. The author understands that passage from place and story to spirituality. He knows that we often need a "prompt" to lead into prayer.

The Franciscans—especially those who minister and work in the lands touched by Jesus, Mary, and the first followers of Christ—are pleased to share this wise pilgrim guide's faith, love and friendship with you on your pilgrimage.

Greg Friedman, OFM
Washington, D.C.
January 2020

PREFACE

·······

A new guide to the Holy Land? We welcome it! We never tire of deepening the mystery of discovering—through others' eyes—new perspectives and meanings.

The diary of the fourth-century pilgrim Egeria is just the first page of a book that has no end because it is enriched every year by new voices of amazed pilgrims who will continue to add to it and will take their places in an uninterrupted line of those who render homage to the sources of faith and of the Church.

Recent editions of "Guides to the Holy Land" update the tireless work of architects and archeologists who in recent decades have confirmed the contents of the two-thousand-year tradition of the Church. Exegetical and historical-biblical research about these places has added pages we cannot ignore that allow us to reach another level of meaningful approach to the Jesus of the Gospels.

Scholarly work still in progress encompasses all of the Holy Land: It is like the lofty, steady flight of an eagle who scrutinizes the mountain heights, the courses of rivers, the valleys, and what the ground still conceals below.

Following the traditional path—*lectio, meditatio, scrutatio, oratio-contemplatio*—Vincenzo Peroni visits every shrine and sanctuary in the Holy Land, leading us on "a journey of contemplation and prayer, a walking spiritual retreat, an occasion for conversion and renewal of life."

In every holy site, we are guided by a biblical text that makes us contemporaries of what Jesus experienced in that specific place through a simple but complete mystagogy (interpretation of the mystery) that includes pertinent references to the Old Testament—mysteries that were first actualized in the community of disciples and then in the life of the Church. We are personally urged to make the "external journey become an interior journey: a holy journey!... Remove my unbelief and lead me to say, 'My Lord and my God.'" This is only one of the prayers that the pilgrim will repeat.

It is helpful to know that the idea for this book also came about from the words of Pope Francis: "Do we listen to Jesus each day in the Gospel?... Jesus's word is the most nourishing food for the soul: It nourishes our souls, it nourishes our faith! I suggest that each day you take a few minutes and read a nice passage of the Gospel."

That same advice can be addressed to the pilgrim who travels to the Holy Land: Informed by scholarly guidebooks about the history and the art of each holy site, do not forget to take this small book with you so that you can repeat this prayer.

Seek me, Lord, and teach me to seek you.

Find me, Lord, and give me the joy of finding you.

Come into my house, Lord, and make me dwell in your presence.

Touch my heart, Lord, and make me able to love.

The pilgrimage through the Holy Land will be even more of a "holy journey" if, in addition to having us encounter Jesus, it will lead us to encounter the Virgin his Mother and to ask ourselves, "How does Mary forge a dialogue between history and the Word of God? Between daily life and the Gospel?"

I heartily support what the author aims at with his book through the grace he has abundantly drawn from his own pilgrimages and his graciousness in sharing with us some jewels unearthed from the "rich mine" of the Holy Land. At the Dominus Flevit (the Church on the Mount of Olives), for example, he says, "Let us ask Jesus to teach us to weep." Doesn't Pope

Francis denounce the fact that contemporary human beings have lost the capacity to weep? Here we can recover that capacity! Here, with hearts purified through tears, we can dare to ask, "Lord, allow me to enter the dialogue between you and your Father."

It is appropriate to conclude with the words Father Vincenzo addresses to the pilgrim at the end of the journey: "Take charge of your life and live like a mature and responsible human being. Enough of this life in which you have always been served! It is up to you now to take hold of your life and begin to live responsibly. Get busy!"

Bishop Pierbattista Pizzaballa, OFM
Custos of the Holy Land 2004-2016
Jerusalem, September 14, 2015
Feast of the Exaltation of the Holy Cross

INTRODUCTION

·······

The opportunity for a journey through the land of Jesus is so unique and valuable that it cannot be squandered. In fact, for a Christian it is not simply *a* journey, it is *the* journey. It is of course a physical journey with all of our senses in contact with the external world, but little by little it can turn into an interior journey until it becomes a holy journey. This journey leads to the transformative encounter with the Lord Jesus through our experience of his presence in the incarnation at Nazareth and in Bethlehem; his proximity in Galilee; his sharing of daily human life in Cana, Jericho, and Jerusalem; his total self-gift in the Eucharist at the Last Supper; his death on the cross at Golgotha; the definitive victory of his resurrection at the Holy Sepulcher.

It is appropriate to have a reliable guide to learn to know and love the Holy Land; it is useful to know some history and the testimony of former pilgrims; and it is valuable to gather archeological data. But what is decisive is our attentive and prayerful listening to the Gospel. Let Jesus speak through the facts and the words of the Gospel. This means "seeing Jesus" as he dwells in and walks through this land, as he encounters the everyday life of human beings and their dramatic and fascinating stories. Let us allow Jesus to engage in conversation with us in the silence of contemplation and prayer.

This book originates from a simple desire: to offer an accessible and practical tool to pilgrims who want to make their journey through the Holy Land one of contemplation and prayer, a walking spiritual retreat, an occasion for conversion and renewal of life.

There are numerous guides available that are, of course, comprehensive and valuable, dedicated to presenting the places of Jesus's homeland. Their texts for meditation on the Word of God are enough to fill entire libraries. This book, which you can carry along with you, is instead a collection of short presentations of reflection and prayer on the "sanctuaries" that preserve the fundamental mysteries of Jesus's life.

Each presentation consists of a Gospel passage, a short meditation, some questions for personal reflection and examination of life, and then a prayer.

The meditations, which have a colloquial tone, are actually transcriptions of reflections and homilies I have delivered during the course of pilgrimages I have led in recent years (often dictated in various situations of standing along the road or in the shade of a plant). I have chosen not to edit the texts in order to maintain the immediacy of communication, even if this comes at the expense of literary elegance at times.

My hope is that pilgrims, taking this small book out of a backpack in moments of silence and solitude that are so vital on a pilgrimage, may be guided to "let themselves be touched by Jesus."

Leaders and directors of Holy Land pilgrimages may also find in this book further inspiration and suggestions to enrich their service.

Those who have returned from a pilgrimage and those who have not yet planned a pilgrimage may discover in this simple instrument an unobtrusive companion for a personal journey of prayer.

Vincenzo Peroni

I
· · · · · · ·
NAZARETH
The Annunciation

From the Gospel according to Luke (1:26-38)

In the sixth month the angel Gabriel was sent by God to a town in Galilee called Nazareth, to a virgin engaged to a man whose name was Joseph, of the house of David. The virgin's name was Mary. And he came to her and said, "Greetings, favored one! The Lord is with you." But she was much perplexed by his words and pondered what sort of greeting this might be. The angel said to her, "Do not be afraid, Mary, for you have found favor with God. And now, you will conceive in your womb and bear a son, and you will name him Jesus. He will be great, and will be called the Son of the Most High, and the Lord God will give to him the throne of his ancestor David. He will reign over the house of Jacob forever, and of his kingdom there will be no end." Mary said to the angel, "How can this be, since I am a virgin?" The angel said to her, "The Holy Spirit will come upon you, and the power of the Most High will overshadow you; therefore the child to be born will be holy; he will be called Son of God. And now, your relative Elizabeth in her old age has also conceived a son; and this is the sixth month for her who was said to be barren. For nothing will be impossible with God." Then Mary said, "Here am I, the servant of the Lord; let it be with me according to your word." Then the angel departed from her.

Meditation

The most genuine reaction in such a holy place is, of course, amazement and silence, but in order for that silence and amazement to have their full meaning, we need to listen to these words.

We find ourselves in a unique place here in Nazareth: It is the exact place that God chose, in his infinite wisdom and mercy, in which to meet human beings in a definitive way.

Here, once and for all, after some dramatic failures in earlier history, God's desire and human beings' desire come together.

Here God's yes to humanity and humanity's yes to God are joined in an invincible alliance.

We can be stunned by the sense of fulfillment and beauty that emanates from this place. If we wanted to review, even briefly, all the history of salvation starting with creation, we would realize how much God is moved by his great desire to reach human beings and bring them into communion with himself; we would see that human beings, despite the deep nostalgia in their hearts to be in communion with God, too often have gone elsewhere to seek consolation for themselves and have repeatedly betrayed God. But God, even more tenaciously (we could say even more stubbornly), chased them until he reached them here, through Mary's flesh.

Here, thanks to the young woman who made herself available during his visitation, God permanently united himself to the flesh of human beings—the flesh that the Word of God assumed in Mary's womb, which, in the mystery of God, in the mystery of the Trinity, becomes resurrected flesh.

The Word of God, the second Person of the most Holy Trinity, God himself, in his holiness and omnipotence, chooses to enter into my flesh, to make it his, to take it into himself, and to unite it definitively to himself. In the flesh that he assumed in Mary's womb, Jesus takes each of us to himself and entrusts us to the Father in a welcoming communion that nothing can break apart—except our freedom to leave it.

In this place, then, we want to learn from Mary's yes and God's yes: God continues to renew his yes. He is in love with human beings and wants to reach them; he desires their salvation but does not impose it on them; he waits for people's freely offered, deliberate, and mature yes, even if it is weak. We are aware of the many times we have said yes and then, unfortunately, compromised that yes through our weakness, our sin. God does not give up; he is not put off by our weakness and our sin. What interests him is the depth and fervor of our hearts. This is the grace we can ask for in this place: that our hearts, our capacity for choosing the good, freely choose God despite our weakness, and perhaps precisely through our weakness. My flesh, as well as my life, is precious in God's sight. This means that every moment of our existence, every breath, every decision, every gesture, every authentic act can be lived out only from the perspective of communion with God, because in his eyes our every breath, desire, gesture, and relationship are precious.

We attribute a wonderful title to Mary in the Loreto Litany of the Blessed Virgin Mary, the title of *Ianua coeli*, the "Gate of Heaven." It can certainly refer to the fact that Mary opens the portal of paradise to us, but if we consider it more closely this title actually finds its reality here more truly, because it is in this very place that Mary became the Gate of Heaven; it is through her that heaven, God himself, was able to enter the earth. The heavens had been closed because of the sin of Adam and Eve: An enormous rupture between God and human beings had occurred. It had been necessary that a young woman make herself available through her choice of complete openness for heaven to be able to dwell on earth. From that moment, precisely in this place, heaven has now come down to earth, and earth is destined for heaven. Highlighting this truth opens up for us a perspective of consolation and hope. There may be many things that disturb us, that cause us to struggle, but the certitude that heaven has now come down to earth and the earth is intended to be heaven is of great comfort and hope.

We could linger a long time on the dialogue between the archangel and Mary, which takes the shape of a perfect dialogue of prayer, but it is enough to highlight certain features. Above all, it becomes clear how Mary demonstrates her humanity and her mindset. In the course of the dialogue with the angel, she asks questions, but she does so humbly, by listening for the answers and accepting them. She does not ask with the attitude of someone who assumes, "I already know the answers," and she does not ask the angel questions that cast doubt on his affirmations so as to escape her accountability more easily. No! The questions Mary addresses to the angel, in light of his great and surprising announcement, are a sign of her openness to deeper revelation because of her desire to consent to God's will in a more conscious way.

This is what our prayer should be like, an authentic dialogue with God in which we allow ourselves to be prodded by God. What God wants to communicate to us often disturbs us, unsettles us, but we must not run away; rather we should be strong before him, with the intention and humility of welcoming in the depth of our hearts what God is asking and consent to it.

Mary is reached by a word; she welcomes that word, and it becomes flesh in her life.

The second feature to highlight is that each time we hear the word of God, if we listen with docility and consent to that word through obedience in our flesh, we are then allowing the mystery of the Incarnation to be extended in history, because it is the Word of God who takes flesh in the flesh of our existence. We too can become little *gates to heaven* for humanity.

How often we complain about how things are going for us; we can have the impression that everything is moving in the opposite direction regarding doing God's will. Perhaps instead of complaining about what is happening, we should focus on what is happening within us.

Those of us who are Christians and have the grace to hear the word of the Gospel, which is truth, become *gates of heaven* when we consent, through our flesh, to the Word of God once again dwelling in humanity's history.

PERSONAL REFLECTION

I see Mary welcoming the angel's announcement; I quietly listen to their dialogue with amazement, and I ask myself:

1. Do I allow myself be surprised by a visit from God that comes to me through the Gospel?
2. Is my listening docile, attentive, full of faith, and obedient? Or do I instead let my emotions, my conjectures, and my fears take precedence?
3. Do I sense the Lord's gaze on my life, his desire to unite me to himself in a genuine embrace of communion and love?
4. Does my prayer arise from listening to the Word of God who wants to become flesh in my life? Does prayer transform me, making me consent to the choice for good that the Lord reveals to me?

PRAYER

Lord, I adore the Mystery of the Incarnation;
I bless the faithfulness of your love;
I celebrate your gaze of tenderness on my weakness.

Wrap me, O Lord, with your shadow;
fill me with your sweet presence;
transform me through the power of your Spirit.

And you, Mary, Mother of the Creator,
Gate of Heaven, tabernacle of the divine presence,
overcome the resistances in my listening,
in my heart, and in my will.

Make me docile to God's visitation;
train all my faculties to repeat with you,
"let it be with me according to your word."

2

· · · · · · ·

EIN KAREM
The Visitation

FROM THE GOSPEL ACCORDING TO LUKE (1:39-58)

In those days Mary set out and went with haste to a Judean town in the hill country, where she entered the house of Zechariah and greeted Elizabeth. When Elizabeth heard Mary's greeting, the child leaped in her womb. And Elizabeth was filled with the Holy Spirit and exclaimed with a loud cry, "Blessed are you among women, and blessed is the fruit of your womb. And why has this happened to me, that the mother of my Lord comes to me? For as soon as I heard the sound of your greeting, the child in my womb leaped for joy. And blessed is she who believed that there would be a fulfillment of what was spoken to her by the Lord." And Mary said,

"My soul magnifies the Lord,

and my spirit rejoices in God my Savior,

for he has looked with favor on the lowliness of his servant.

Surely, from now on all generations will call me blessed;

for the Mighty One has done great things for me, and holy is his name.

His mercy is for those who fear him from generation to generation.

He has shown strength with his arm; he has scattered the proud in the thoughts of their hearts.

He has brought down the powerful from their thrones, and lifted up the lowly;

He has filled the hungry with good things, and sent the rich away empty.

He has helped his servant Israel, in remembrance of his mercy, according to the promise he made to our ancestors, to Abraham and to his descendants forever."

And Mary remained with her about three months and then returned to her home.

Now the time came for Elizabeth to give birth, and she bore a son. Her neighbors and relatives heard that the Lord had shown his great mercy to her, and they rejoiced with her.

MEDITATION

Christian tradition places the location of the house of Zechariah and Elizabeth here at Ein Karem. It is the house in which Mary stayed shortly after receiving the angel's announcement.

Luke offers us a theological reading of Mary's journey, and through that new reading he wants us to understand who Mary is at that moment, but above all, who the One in her womb is. Mary leaves Nazareth immediately after the Annunciation, immediately after the Incarnation of the Word, with Jesus in her womb.

Having learned from the angel that a relative living far away was already six months pregnant, Mary leaves to go visit her. Why does she come here to this relative so far away? Mary's visit to Elizabeth conceals a great act of charity. What act is that?

The most immediate interpretation suggests that Mary came to help out an elderly cousin who needed assistance. However, it is at the very least improbable that a person would travel over ninety miles with the Son of God in her womb just to help a woman with household chores. Elizabeth could have easily been assisted by her neighbors. In addition, Luke tells us that after three months, Mary leaves before Elizabeth gives birth, so she apparently did not travel all that distance to be present for the most significant days of the childbirth itself.

Mary did not come to help Elizabeth in her time of need. She came to bring Jesus.

This is the true charitable act of a Christian. Before all the other useful and wonderful acts of charity in which we spend our time well, the genuinely great charitable act that a Christian can do is to bring Jesus, because there is no greater good that we can present to others. We can perform wonderful and grandiose works, but if they are void of Jesus, what good are they? All the greatest works we can perform end with us and are over, but if we bring Jesus, he remains.

Mary goes to a woman who can understand the mystery that is occurring in her womb because Elizabeth herself was the object of divine mercy: The Lord has done great things for both of them! Both of them experience extraordinary pregnancies: One woman was barren and the other became supernaturally pregnant without the involvement of a man.

The Hebrew Scriptures tell us another important event occurred in Ein Karem: the transporting of the Ark of the Covenant to the city of David, which is described in 2 Samuel 6. It is a wonderful, specific description along the same lines the Gospel writer Luke describes Mary's journey to Elizabeth's house. If we read the accounts of these two episodes in parallel, despite their distance in time, we become aware of many points of similarity.

There is a very specific point of contact between the narration of the transporting of the Ark and the narration of Mary's meeting with Elizabeth. When Mary arrives at Ein Karem, she greets her cousin Elizabeth. She was full of the Holy Spirit, who came upon her during the Incarnation of the Word, and the Spirit in her communicates to Elizabeth and the child in her womb who then both become prophets. After all, how would Elizabeth know that Mary is the "mother of my Lord" if it were not the Holy Spirit who inspired her?

"As soon as I heard the sound of your greeting, the child in my womb leaped for joy." In Luke's Greek text and the Greek text of the Septuagint's version of 2 Samuel, the same word, *skirtao*, is used to describe the leaping for joy of John the Baptist in Elizabeth's womb and to narrate David's dance of joy as the Ark of the Covenant is being transported. *Skirtao* is also used in Psalm114:4 to describe mountains and hills in the desert of Judea poetically leaping or skipping like lambs as the people enter the Promised Land behind the Ark. The same word is used for the joyful leaping in these three episodes widely separated in time but very closely linked.

When the people enter into the Promised Land with the Ark of the Covenant, creation exults in God's visitation; when David transports the Ark of the Covenant that holds the Tablets of the Law, representing the presence of the Lord, he dances before it with all his might. John the Baptist, the tiny baby in Elizabeth's womb, leaps for joy at Mary's arrival because he recognizes in Mary the new Ark of the Covenant: Jesus is inside her, and he is the new and eternal covenant.

When we celebrate the Eucharist and take up the chalice, we say it is the cup of the new and eternal covenant. Jesus is the new and eternal covenant that Mary brings as a gift to Zechariah, Elizabeth, and John.

Why is this journey so important? Because Zechariah and Elizabeth represent the last of the Old Testament people who are awaiting the Messiah. Mary is instead the new woman, the new Israel, who presents herself to the old Israel and says, "The fullness of time has come; God has been faithful to his promise." The two children recognize each other while in their mothers' wombs: John, the last and greatest of the prophets, and Jesus, the fulfillment of all the prophecies.

When we celebrate John the Baptist in the liturgy, we say that not only did he prophesy but he also announced the presence of the Messiah in the world. No other prophet could have pointed the Messiah out as being present. On the banks of the river Jordan, John said, "Behold the Lamb of God; it is truly he, and he has now come."

Mary bursts forth with the Magnificat, the canticle we celebrate every evening of the liturgical year. How is this canticle structured? It takes the form of a celebration of what God does. If we read it carefully, it is not structured as a prayer but as a narrative, a profession of faith. The words of the Magnificat express ongoing action to affirm that this is always what God does; this is how he acts in all of history. This is his style: He turns things around to bring his promises to fulfillment.

Pope Benedict XVI, commenting on the Magnificat, said many historical theories have been formulated to interpret the development of nations and understand how the history of humanity unfolded, but even the ones that seem the most likely and capable of interpreting history have proven to be flawed. Only one reading of history does not break down over time, and it is the Magnificat. This is how God directs history. This is how God habitually acts with humanity: He brings his promise to fulfillment.

In Nazareth, we saw the place in which the Word of God became flesh in Mary's womb. We learned there that every time we listen to the word of God we host Jesus within us and, in a certain sense, we thereby extend the mystery of the Incarnation within us.

If we have this openness, God brings to fulfillment his work in our lives; our very existence becomes a work of charity because through our flesh, our thoughts, our actions, and our relationships, we bring Jesus to our brothers and sisters. And wherever Jesus enters the scene, there is joy, true joy that nothing can take away, not even misfortunes or hardships. That joy is authentic because Jesus has arrived, and he is the fullness of every good for human beings.

PERSONAL REFLECTION

I see Mary running to Elizabeth to bring her the announcement of the Incarnation. I see Elizabeth and John exulting for joy as they recognize a visit by the Ark of the Covenant. I ask myself:

1. Do I experience an urgency to give Jesus to my brothers and sisters?
2. Do I recognize and celebrate the great works the Lord has accomplished in history?

3. Do I confidently await the fulfillment of God's promises?
4. Do I joyfully celebrate God's faithfulness despite the struggles and the contradictions in history?

PRAYER

The Canticle of the Blessed Virgin Mary (Luke 1:46-45)

My soul magnifies the Lord,

and my spirit rejoices in God my Savior,

for he has looked with favor on the lowliness of his servant.

Surely, from now on all generations will call me blessed;

for the Mighty One has done great things for me, and holy is his name.

His mercy is for those who fear him from generation to generation.

He has shown strength with his arm; he has scattered the proud in the thoughts of their hearts.

He has brought down the powerful from their thrones, and lifted up the lowly.

He has filled the hungry with good things, and sent the rich away empty.

He has helped his servant Israel, in remembrance of his mercy,

according to the promise he made to our ancestors, to Abraham and to his descendants forever.

Glory be to the Father, the Son, and the Holy Spirit,

As it was in the beginning, is now, and ever shall be.

3

BETHLEHEM
The Nativity

From the Gospel according to Luke (2:1-21)

In those days a decree went out from Emperor Augustus that all the world should be registered. This was the first registration and was taken while Quirinius was governor of Syria. All went to their own towns to be registered. Joseph also went from the town of Nazareth in Galilee to Judea, to the city of David called Bethlehem, because he was descended from the house and family of David. He went to be registered with Mary, to whom he was engaged and who was expecting a child. While they were there, the time came for her to deliver her child. And she gave birth to her firstborn son and wrapped him in bands of cloth, and laid him in a manger, because there was no place for them in the inn.

In that region there were shepherds living in the fields, keeping watch over their flock by night. Then an angel of the Lord stood before them, and the glory of the Lord shone around them, and they were terrified. But the angel said to them, "Do not be afraid; for see—I am bringing you good news of great joy for all the people: to you is born this day in the city of David a Savior, who is the Messiah, the Lord. This will be a sign for you: you will find a child wrapped in bands of cloth and lying in a manger." And suddenly there was with the angel a multitude of the heavenly host, praising God and saying,

"Glory to God in the highest heaven,
and on earth peace among those whom he favors!"

When the angels had left them and gone into heaven, the shepherds said to one another, "Let us go now to Bethlehem and see this thing that has taken place, which the Lord has made known to us." So they went with haste and found Mary and Joseph, and the child lying in the manger. When they saw this, they made known what had been told them about this child; and all who heard it were amazed at what the shepherds told them. But Mary treasured all these words and pondered them in her heart. The shepherds returned, glorifying and praising God for all they had heard and seen, as it had been told them.

After eight days had passed, it was time to circumcise the child; and he was called Jesus, the name given by the angel before he was conceived in the womb.

MEDITATION

This passage is from the second chapter of the Gospel of Luke. Let's take note of the many theological details in this passage that enable us to review the event of Jesus's birth in depth. These concrete details manifest the mystery of God and his action for the salvation of human beings.

We are told about an important historical fact here: The Roman government had ordered a census in which people had to be listed according to their family's original hometown. Therefore, Joseph and Mary, who was pregnant, went to Bethlehem from Nazareth. We are seeing here the fulfillment of ancient promises.

Mary gave birth to her first-born son and "wrapped him in bands of cloth, and laid him in a manger, because there was no place for them in the inn." In the short passage above from Luke the word *manger* is repeated three times, which points to an important emphasis. If the Gospel writer is emphasizing that the baby was lying in manger, that means there is something significant here. What is ordinarily put in a manger? Something that is to be eaten, so we are being told that the child will, in the future, need to be eaten.

As you walk around the Grotto of Nativity at Bethlehem, you will observe icons in which the artists represent the manger in the shape of a tomb. This baby has just been born, but there is death in his future that will make him become food for all.

Jesus, speaking of his death one day, says he is like a grain of wheat that falls into the ground, dies, and produces much fruit; he will become a full-grown sheaf that is then used to produce bread. Bethlehem, in fact, means "House of Bread." This child is like a grain of wheat that will be put into the ground when he dies to become food to nourish his friends.

In addition, this was the location of the visit by the Magi. Remember the three gifts? Though they symbolize divinity and majesty, myrrh represents the fact that this body will be anointed for death.

After giving birth to Jesus, Mary does something rather normal: She wraps him in swaddling clothes, but even swaddling clothes recall the burial shroud in a tomb.

Jesus was born at night, and this was not accidental. Sacred Scripture tells us about several nights in the history of salvation. The first great night involves creation when everything comes forth from dark nothingness. God makes his covenant with Abraham at night. God, through his mighty arm, delivers his people from the slavery of Egypt at night. People were awaiting the night of the Messiah, and Jesus was born at night.

Several shepherds were tending their sheep in the countryside that night. Let's take a look at these shepherds because they are quite interesting and can offer us some valuable information. These shepherds are not like those nice figurines that we put in manger scenes or like those described poetically in so many of our Christmas songs.

These men had a tricky social situation. Because of their work, they were constantly in contact with only their animals and cut off from human relationships. They had to tend to their flocks mostly away from inhabited areas, so this prevented them from participating regularly at prayer in the synagogue.

This undercut their participation in the life of the religious community and, in a certain sense, was excluding them from the opportunity for salvation. In brief, they were nocturnal people wrapped in the shadow of obscurity and without light.

Far away from inhabited places, they had one task to perform for their flocks in the fields. The Gospel says, they were "living in the fields, keeping watch over their flock by night." They were "living *in the fields*," that is, not inside tents, which would have prevented them from seeing other things outdoors. All night long they were "*keeping watch*," so their work forced them to look to the horizon for the rising sun, hoping in the meantime that no one would come to steal their sheep.

Their work actually saved them because it taught them the fundamental attitude of vigilance, of peering into the darkness, of peering into the night, so when the angels came to announce the birth of the Savior they went to the shepherds first. From the dominant religious point of view, these men were exiled from society and considered unworthy of salvation, but they were the first to receive the angel's message.

When the angel appeared to the shepherds, the glory of the Lord surrounded them with light.

These men of darkness and gloom, men of the night, are now wrapped in light. They were afraid. The angel tells them, "Do not be afraid; for see—I am bringing you good news of great joy." The technical meaning here is, "I am evangelizing you; I am bringing you good news."

The angel says, "To you is born this day...a Savior, who is the Messiah, the Lord."

This announcement summarizes all the theological titles that the Old Testament had reserved for the arrival of the Messiah. The angel's announcement is thunderous, tremendous, grandiose, but immediately after it he says, "This will be a sign for you: You will find a child wrapped in bands of cloth, lying in a manger." They will see a small, fragile being wrapped up in swaddling clothes in a manger. Here is the height of power and holiness in the most humble, lowly, and fragile form imaginable.

And then all the angels burst forth into praise of God in the *Gloria*.

The shepherds say, "Let us go now to Bethlehem and see this thing." Wonderful! They heard a message and were also given a sign by which to recognize the child. They say, "Let's go and see," and they will interpret what they see in light of what they heard. "So they went" to see what the angel had told them about.

The shepherds reached the grotto and recounted what the angel had said, announcing the angelic message to those present. They were evangelizing, but whom were they evangelizing? Joseph, Mary, and all the others present.

Mary could have said, "Excuse me, but I know very well who this baby is. I gave birth to him, I know how he appeared in my womb, and I can tell you all about that." Mary is instead silent, listening to the message of the shepherds, and she lets herself be evangelized.

This is an impressive attitude that gives us valuable spiritual instruction, because no one can presume to know the Gospel enough. Each of us needs to receive it and be evangelized repeatedly.

Even Mary needed a message to help her understand the mystery of this child to whom she had just given birth.

The Gospel writer says, "all who heard it were amazed" (although he does not tell us what choice any of them made). "But Mary treasured all these words and pondered them in her heart." The word *But* here tell us that she was not like the others. She was the mother of this child and had a special relationship with her son and with the mystery of God that was being manifested. "Mary treasured all these things"—in Greek, *tà remata panta*—means that she was meditating on the words and actions of what happened, on the shepherds' words and on the birth itself.

"Pondered"—in Greek, *syn-ballo*—means putting things together. In her heart Mary was making the connection between the birth of her son and the shepherds' words; their words were the explanation, and her son was the confirmation of those words.

We should notice that Mary is uniting word and flesh together in her heart here. Isn't this the same thing that we saw in Nazareth? Isn't this the extension of the mystery of Nazareth? When we connect God's word with events in our lives, we are doing exactly what Mary did.

Once more we need to let ourselves to be caught up in amazement and in contemplation, but we must also learn to take on the attitudes displayed here. The shepherds' attitude is one of vigilance, of those who know how to scan the horizon in the darkness, believing the light will finally arise. Mary's attitude teaches us to allow the Gospel to reach us and interpret the events in our lives, so that our whole lives have a sense of the presence of God.

PERSONAL REFLECTION

I look at the Grotto of Nativity in Bethlehem and re-examine the scene of Jesus's birth. I observe the actions of Mary and Joseph; I watch the angels and follow the shepherds' path; I listen to the words and the dialogues. And I ask myself:

1. Does the fragility of the Baby Jesus touch me just emotionally, or does it lead me to see God in action in the history of mankind in a profound way?

2. Do Christmas poems or the drama of love that takes place in the hiddenness of a grotto move me more now? How deeply conscious am I that God himself, the Holy and Omnipotent One, wrapped himself in the fragility of human flesh for my salvation?

3. Do I know how to keep watch at night like the shepherds did? Will I persevere in scanning the horizon where the true sun of humanity arises, the true Morning Star that never sets and gives salvation, Christ Jesus? And do I await my full salvation as a gift of grace from him?

4. Like Mary, do I connect history and the word of God? Do I connect daily life and the Gospel?

5. Like the shepherds, do I make the effort to journey, to seek, to go

see? Do I proclaim with amazement and wonder what was proclaimed to me and what I have seen?

PRAYER

I see you wrapped in swaddling clothes, O Lord Jesus;
I see you lying in a manger;
I see you fragile and helpless;
and I adore you!

I see you as a tiny baby, O Lord Jesus;
I see you still and silent;
I see you engulfed by the night of the world
and I adore you!

Through the eyes of Mary, your mother,
I recognize you as the Son of God;
through her heart, I contemplate your Mystery;
through her humble obedience, I embrace your presence;
and I adore you!

Together with the shepherds, I run towards you,
O Light that breaks up the darkness;
with their thirst for salvation, I trust the Gospel;
with their amazement, I praise the greatness of God;
and I adore you!

Together with the Holy Magi,
I offer you the gifts of my faith and love;
with a desire like theirs to know you,
I prostrate myself in your presence;
with wisdom like theirs, I acknowledge you are the truth;
and I adore you!

4

CAPERNAUM

Jesus Begins His Ministry

From the Gospel according to Mark 1:21-39

They went to Capernaum; and when the sabbath came, he entered the synagogue and taught. They were astounded at his teaching, for he taught them as one having authority, and not as the scribes. Just then there was in their synagogue a man with an unclean spirit, and he cried out, "What have you to do with us, Jesus of Nazareth? Have you come to destroy us? I know who you are, the Holy One of God." But Jesus rebuked him, saying, "Be silent, and come out of him!" And the unclean spirit, convulsing him and crying with a loud voice, came out of him. They were all amazed, and they kept on asking one another, "What is this? A new teaching—with authority! He commands even the unclean spirits, and they obey him." At once his fame began to spread throughout the surrounding region of Galilee.

As soon as they left the synagogue, they entered the house of Simon and Andrew, with James and John. Now Simon's mother-in-law was in bed with a fever, and they told him about her at once. He came and took her by the hand and lifted her up. Then the fever left her, and she began to serve them.

That evening, at sundown, they brought to him all who were sick or possessed with demons. And the whole city was gathered around the door. And he cured many who were sick with various diseases, and cast out many demons; and he would not permit the demons to speak, because they knew him. In the morning, while it was still very dark, he got up and went out to a deserted place, and there he prayed. And Simon and his companions hunted for him. When they found him, they said to him, "Everyone is searching for you."

He answered, "Let us go on to the neighboring towns, so that I may proclaim the message there also; for that is what I came out to do." And he went throughout Galilee, proclaiming the message in their synagogues and casting out demons.

At Capernaum inside the synagogue (the place in which Jesus promised the Eucharist), we can reread and meditate on John 6 and, in front of Peter's house, on the passage about the healing of the paralytic (Mk 2:1-12).

MEDITATION

Jesus arrives in Capernaum on the Sabbath and enters the synagogue for prayer. He abides by the sequence of the Jewish service. During prayer he gives a teaching, and there are at least two reactions to his teaching.

All are amazed and fascinated since there is something new in his teaching because he speaks with authority and credibility. He is not like the others who give the impression of having learned the teaching by heart without it having an impact on their lives. Jesus puts his whole self into what he teaches, and for that reason he is credible.

There is also another reaction, however: that of an unclean spirit who is enslaving a man. The unclean spirit is aware of what is at stake and asks Jesus, "Have you come to destroy us?" He is saying, "Have you come to destroy the kingdom of Satan with your authority, clarity, and the truth of your teaching?" Jesus makes him be quiet.

"I know who you are, the Holy One of God." Jesus prevents him from speaking. Why does Jesus stop Satan from saying who he is? Satan has a clear understanding of who God is; he knows very well who Jesus is. Satan knows the content of faith perfectly, but he is lacking one thing: love. Faith does not consist solely in precise, cerebral, and theologically perfect knowledge; faith involves a commitment of one's life to a relationship of love with the Lord. This is what Satan is lacking. Merely knowing the truth, without love, can even be perilous. Jesus prevents the unclean spirit from speaking because the people there are not yet ready to receive the revelation of his divinity.

Jesus finishes the exorcism and the Gospel tells us that the unclean spirit, "convulsing [the possessed man] and crying with a loud voice, came out of him." That leaves an impression. Mark, who writes straightforwardly, does not want to present dramatic film scenes; that is a typical sign of Satan's work. Jesus is freeing that man, so before leaving Satan makes a final attempt to keep the man enslaved, as if he were asking, "Are you really sure you want to stay with him? Do you realize that staying with him will cost you a lot of suffering and heartbreak? Think about it: do I really need to leave you alone?"

This happens many times to us too when, after a retreat, a time of prayer, a conference, or a pilgrimage to the Holy Land, we sense that our lives need to change. And then we think, "I really have to commit myself now; I need to start following the Lord the way I know I should." But then immediately something happens that can give us the feeling that being with Jesus will cost us something, a feeling that wants to fool us into believing that the Lord is opposed to our joy. We need to be vigilant against this.

Everyone in the synagogue was filled with fear. They were amazed and fascinated, but we are not told if they followed Jesus after this or not.

Then Jesus and his companions left and went to Simon's house. The Gospel tells us they went to the house of the brothers Simon and Andrew along with James and John, two other brothers Jesus had called on the shores of the lake. Here we have two pairs of brothers, but what counts now is no longer their blood relationship; what counts is that the first pair of brothers and the second pair are related to Jesus. This is a new company now, a new family based on a relationship with Jesus Christ that surpasses even blood ties.

Simon's mother-in-law was in bed with a fever "and they told him about her at once." This is beautiful because it is a perfect description of intercessory prayer. They did not say to Jesus, "Heal her because she is sick."

Instead they spoke about her, they presented her to him. He takes care of the situation; he knows what he has to do. The Gospel says, "He *came* and *took her* by the hand and *lifted* her *up*." These three verbs summarize all the work of salvation by Jesus. Isn't it true that Jesus *came* to humanity? By taking on our flesh, hasn't he *taken* onto himself all our fragility, just the way he is touching the mother-in-law and taking on her sickness? And he *lifts* her *up*, he makes her rise up. Incarnation, passion, death, and resurrection—these events encompass all of Jesus's work. We can say this episode is a paradigm: From this point on we know how Jesus will act.

That night, after sunset, the people brought him all who were sick and possessed by demons. The whole city had come and camped outside the door. He healed many who were sick and cast out many demons (notice it does not say "all"), but he did not allow the demons to speak because they knew who he was. It was not up to them to reveal that truth because demons are deceivers, so even if they speak the truth they would not be credible.

He rose early in the morning when it was still dark and retired to a deserted place to pray there. That makes an impression! Jesus prays! How many times do we ask, "With everything I have to do, with all my trials and tribulations, why do I have to pray? Besides, isn't my work also my prayer? Aren't all the things I do prayers too?" We offer a lot of reasons to explain that we have no time, that we are tired and do not have the energy. The single thing that unmasks all our tricks and the things we are hiding is the answer to why should we pray: because Jesus was praying. The verb in the imperfect tense means, among other things, that it was a continuous action. He was continuing to pray even though he had spent an entire sabbath day that was exhausting for him: He had preached, he had met people, he had performed healing. He could have slept in for a while. Instead he robs himself of sleep at night so that he could retire alone on the mountain to pray.

Why does Jesus pray? He needs to pray to remain in the truth; he needs to pray to keep being himself. He cannot be himself without being before the Father's face. Do you remember the wonderful passage from John's Prologue? "In the beginning was the Word, and the Word was with God, and the Word was God" (John 1:1). What does this mean? "In the beginning" does not just mean before everything else; it also means at the origin. Before the origin of all things, the Word was with God, that is, the Word was gazing on the face of God. From all eternity in the mystery of the Trinity, the stance of the Word, the second Person of the Trinity, the Son, is to gaze on the Father's face. When Jesus became incarnated, he did not lose that standing, and it was necessary to bring even the flesh he had assumed into that standing too. So prayer served to bring himself, his humanity, his flesh, before the face of God so that everything might be before the face of God.

The disciples, still focused on success and consensus, ran after him and told him there was a crowd of people waiting for him. How did Jesus respond? "Let us go on to the neighboring towns." Having gazed on the Father's face, he now had the liberty to say, "Seeing these people again is not what I came for. I need to proclaim the Kingdom of God and to tell everyone in the neighboring villages, too, about the Father. That is what is urgent for me. If I had stayed comfortably on my mat to rest from yesterday's fatigue and had not met with the Father, then I could now be enjoying compliments from the city of Capernaum, but that is not useful."

PERSONAL REFLECTION

As I watch Jesus in his daily routine, I learn what is important to him, and I ask myself:

1. Does the fascination I feel for Jesus become transformed into joyful commitment to him?

2. Do I allow Jesus to unmask the deception and falsehoods in me?
3. Do the weariness and adversity that come from faithfulness to the Gospel lead to a desire (=temptation) to distance myself from him?
4. What criteria do I use to evaluate my personal life and the life of my parish or diocese? Success and consensus or truth and charity?

PRAYER

O Lord, let me enter into the dialogue between you and the Father;
inspire me to have a desire for prayer;
make me long for silence.

Make me vigilant, O Lord,
against Satan's temptations;
give me your Spirit of courage so as not to flee
in the face of persecution and adversity;
keep me faithful to your friendship.

O Lord, watch over all my brothers and sisters
and all my friends who are having trials
[It is good to mention here every person who is dear to you by name.]

5

MOUNT OF BEATITUDES

The Sermon on the Mount

From the Gospel according to Matthew (5:1-15)

When Jesus saw the crowds, he went up the mountain; and after he sat down, his disciples came to him. Then he began to speak, and taught them, saying:

"Blessed are the poor in spirit, for theirs is the kingdom of heaven.

Blessed are those who mourn, for they will be comforted.

Blessed are the meek, for they will inherit the earth.

Blessed are those who hunger and thirst for righteousness, for they will be filled.

Blessed are the merciful, for they will receive mercy.

Blessed are the pure in heart, for they will see God.

Blessed are the peacemakers, for they will be called children of God.

Blessed are those who are persecuted for righteousness' sake, for theirs is the kingdom of heaven.

Blessed are you when people revile you and persecute you and utter all kinds of evil against you falsely on my account. Rejoice and be glad, for your reward is great in heaven, for in the same way they persecuted the prophets who were before you.

You are the salt of the earth; but if salt has lost its taste, how can its saltiness be restored? It is no longer good for anything, but is thrown out and trampled under foot. You are the light of the world. A city built on a hill cannot be hid. No one after lighting a lamp puts it under the bushel basket, but on the lampstand, and it gives light to all in the house. In the same way, let your light shine before others, so that they may see your good works and give glory to your Father in heaven."

MEDITATION

St. Paul has a wonderful saying: "Rejoice in the Lord always; again I will say, Rejoice" (Philippians 4:4). He is commanding us to be joyful. Is it even possible to obey that command?

It would seem to be impossible. Paul is being quite specific, however, when he says, "rejoice *in* the Lord." We definitely act at times more foolishly than this: occasions in which we force ourselves and others to be happy, even, unfortunately, people who at that moment have no reason to be happy. At times we even risk introducing that approach into the liturgy. How often we hear a statement such as, "Today is a great feast for us, and we should be happy!" And yet, someone in the congregation may have a broken heart or has recently experienced great wounding or some kind of misfortune. It is not enough to ask them to be joyful; we need to explain to them the reason for that joy.

All of this leads me to say that we need to learn about and know the source of our joy. We need to know where to go to obtain joy even in the midst of tragic situations. We need to realize it is possible to obey Paul's saying, "rejoice always," but only if we hear what he says in full, that is, with the significant phrase "*in the Lord.*"

Let us take a look at the Beatitudes again. They indicate that people can be blessed, happy, and full of joy about a whole series of categories that, in themselves, do not belong to a list of things that bring happiness according to our way of thinking. Those who weep because of their affliction are those who suffer to the point of tears. And then there are the poor in spirit, those who hunger and thirst, those who are persecuted, and so on. We need to understand what the Beatitudes are really all about.

The Fathers of the Church taught us that the Beatitudes are a self-portrait of Jesus. The *categories* of who is blessed point to a portrait of Jesus in his passion and death. The *reasons* for being blessed (because theirs is the kingdom of heaven, because they will be comforted, because they will inherit the earth, etc.) are a portrait of Jesus in his resurrection. The explanation for being blessed does not lie in people's current situation but in the final result (because they will be given the earth, because they will be called children of God, and so on). Jesus is speaking of himself, particularly his passion, death, and resurrection, as he outlines this self-portrait. The *categories* of people and of their blessedness describe Jesus in his passion and death; the *reasons* for their blessedness speak of his resurrection. These eight beatitudes present the features of the face of Jesus.

It is a solemn scene. Jesus, the new Moses, climbs a mountain and, in the classic approach of a Master, "delivers'" the new law that shapes and gives form to the new people of God, the Church.

And how is the Church constituted? In the likeness of Jesus who died and rose again. Jesus begins his self-portrait and, after having said eight times, "Blessed are those who...," he changes the subject being addressed and says, "Blessed are *you*...."

The crowd before him by definition has no configuration; it is amorphous. But his disciples are there close by. He looks at them and says, "Blessed are you when people revile you and persecute you and utter all kinds of evil against you falsely on my account. Rejoice and be glad, for your reward is great in heaven." In other words he is saying, "Blessed are you when you resemble me in my passion, death, and resurrection, when the same thing happens to you that will happen to me in Jerusalem. Then you will have joy."

We have now found the source of our joy. Jesus has taken his love for us so seriously that he faced death and the tomb to rise again, and this is what he has prepared for us. If we truly want to be happy, we only need to share the Passover of Jesus. Only Jesus is the source of joy, and we are happy to the extent that we draw on this source. Should we use another Gospel image? Jesus is the true vine that does the hard work of producing fruit; we bear fruit only if we continue to be grafted into Jesus, the true vine.

What is the Mass? It is the event that makes us contemporaries of the life, death, and resurrection of Jesus. Yes, the Mass is a feast, but it is above all a sacrifice. It is a renewal of the gift that Jesus makes of himself on the cross and in his death and resurrection. To the extent that we nourish ourselves with his death and resurrection, we are joining the feast. The feast is not based on us; it is based on him. The fact that we eat his body and drink his blood—just as Jesus requested in his great discourse on the Bread of Life in the synagogue at Capernaum—means that we are nourishing ourselves on his Passover. That Passover becomes the guarantee that the time in which we are living expands into the spheres of eternity. It allows us to look down from on high at our lives together with his— including, of course, the hard work, the sorrows, the suffering—and to know that the outcome will be victory, salvation, and fullness of joy. Only we Christians have this grace, not because we are better than others but because the Lord has given it to us.

We have the source of joy because Jesus Christ is the truth that allows us to navigate all the circumstances of our lives. That is why the Gospel of Matthew, as it continues with the Sermon on the Mount, records immediately after this the teaching that says, "You are the salt of the earth…. You are the light of the world." It is a very specific teaching. Jesus does not say to his disciples, "How good it would be if you were the salt of the earth; how I wish you were the light of the world and would commit yourselves to that." He is not moralizing but is speaking a word of revelation. It is as if he were saying, "It is precisely so that you could resemble me that I died and rose again, so that you could share my life; therefore, you already are salt and light and are thus capable of giving flavor, of illuminating reality; like salt, you are capable of purifying and preserving everything in its essence."

He says, "You are the salt of the earth and the light of the world." Why "of the earth"? If we turn to the first pages of Genesis, man was formed from the earth. Therefore, to be salt of the earth means that Christians resembling Jesus succeed in bringing real flavor to people's lives. Christians are the ones in history who guard the truth about human beings and their dignity. This is the reason we allow ourselves to say something about political choices, not because we want to be political activists, but because we care about human beings in the name of Jesus Christ. We cannot tell ourselves, "Be quiet and say those things behind closed doors," because in obedience to Jesus Christ we care about our fellow citizens and countrymen. We rebel against that silence and proclaim the truth to everyone about the abuses of human beings. You are the light of the world, but what world is that? The world is the location of the dynamic interaction in relations among people. We Christians, who resemble and belong to Jesus, carry the light of his word into the midst of relationships. We understand that relationships cannot be lived out simply by instinct but according to the truth that comes from God, so it can lead us to salvation.

Here, in this peaceful place, we are with Jesus, knowing that as we remain with him, we will find our joy. Being with Jesus and having our joy in him, we can truly become peacemakers, wherever the word *peace* has the overall meaning of the fullness of God's gifts. We can bring forth the fullness of God's gifts if we let ourselves be indwelt by the presence and consoling companionship of his friendship.

PERSONAL REFLECTION

I listen to Jesus as he reveals himself to the crowd and to his disciples and as he unfolds the mysteries of his Kingdom in outlining the fundamental characteristics of the new people of God.

1. Do I know Jesus? Do I let myself be introduced into his mystery with docility? Do I allow him to reveal his face to me, or do I choose only the features that please me?

2. Where do I find the source of my joy?

3. When I am sad, do I recognize the underlying cause of my sadness?

4. What can I do to live out the Passover in a concrete way?

5. Do I allow Jesus to put to death the "old man" in me so that the "new man" can come forth?

6. Do I feel any responsibility to be salt and light for brothers and sisters—even through my inadequate testimony—so that they too can taste Jesus and let themselves be enlightened by him?

PRAYER

I contemplate your suffering face, Lord;

I contemplate your resurrected face;

I contemplate the mystery of your life and resurrection.

You, Lord, are my joy;

you are the true light of my life;

you are the fullness of meaning for every day.

Unite me, Lord, to your Passover;

unite me to your gift of love;

unite me to yourself, the inexhaustible source of life.

6
· · · · · · ·

LAKE TIBERIAS
Storm on the Sea of Galilee

From the Gospel according to Mark (4:35-41)

> On that day, when evening had come, he said to them, "Let us go across to the other side." And leaving the crowd behind, they took him with them in the boat, just as he was. Other boats were with him.
>
> A great windstorm arose, and the waves beat into the boat, so that the boat was already being swamped. But he was in the stern, asleep on the cushion; and they woke him up and said to him, "Teacher, do you not care that we are perishing?"
>
> He woke up and rebuked the wind, and said to the sea, "Peace! Be still!" Then the wind ceased, and there was a dead calm. He said to them, "Why are you afraid? Have you still no faith?" And they were filled with great awe and said to one another, "Who then is this, that even the wind and the sea obey him?"

MEDITATION

Jesus was asleep. He continued sleeping in the stern of the boat, resting on a cushion. Jesus said that the Son of Man has nowhere to lay his head, and here we are told he only had a cushion. This sleep is different than any other night's sleep because it is a sleep that instantly refers to his death. We are on a large body of water, which in biblical symbolism recalls sin and death, and Jesus is asleep. The disciples wake him up and are angry because they are upset that he is sleeping: "Do you not care that we are perishing?" This is an aggressive question that at times can also be found between the lines in the prayers of Christians when we feel that God is absent from a situation, when things happen that make us ask, "But where is the Lord? Is he perhaps distracted or sleeping and is not interested in us?"

They wake him up. Jesus rises, and the verb for "rise" is typically used of the resurrection. He was sleeping on a cushion; they wake him up and he gets up, and then speaks a word that is a powerful word by the Creator who has power over the forces of nature. "Peace! Be still!" "Peace, be still," is also what Jesus says to us on so many occasions: when we are agitated, when we have thousands of questions, when we continue to complicate our lives all by ourselves and we unfortunately get upset with the Lord. At those times, the Lord tells us, "Peace, be still, stop it; things are already being settled. First of all, do not think that I am sleeping or absent, and then do not accuse me with questions like, 'Where did you go? Are you sleeping? Don't you care about me?' Try instead to turn to me and to recognize my presence."

Of course sometimes the waiting periods are different than we would like; sometimes we have to go through the silence of Holy Saturday, waiting for that third day, the time of the overturning of the death and the tomb. Jesus, however, demonstrating his power over the elements and this body of water in particular, which symbolically recalls sin and death, is saying, "Through my sleep, the sleep of my death, I can also conquer the power that sin and death has over human beings. Why are you so afraid? Do you still not have faith?" The relationship between fear and the lack of faith is clear.

From the Gospel according to Matthew (14:22-33)

Immediately he made the disciples get into the boat and go on ahead to the other side, while he dismissed the crowds. And after he had dismissed the crowds, he went up the mountain by himself to pray. When evening came, he was there alone, but by this time the boat, battered by the waves, was far from the land, for the wind was against them.

And early in the morning he came walking toward them on the sea. But when the disciples saw him walking on the sea, they were terrified, saying, "It is a ghost!" And they cried out in fear.

But immediately Jesus spoke to them and said, "Take heart, it is I; do not be afraid."

Peter answered him, "Lord, if it is you, command me to come to you on the water."

He said, "Come." So Peter got out of the boat, started walking on the water, and came toward Jesus. But when he noticed the strong wind, he became frightened, and beginning to sink, he cried out, "Lord, save me!" Jesus immediately reached out his hand and caught him, saying to him, "You of little faith, why did you doubt?" When they got into the boat, the wind ceased. And those in the boat worshiped him, saying, "Truly you are the Son of God."

MEDITATION

Here in the hills around the lake, Jesus has just preformed the multiplication of the loaves and fishes, which the Gospel writer Matthew recounts, so what does Jesus do now? Jesus seems to be saying, "Let's see if you understand something. I am arranging to send the people home, so go to the lake ahead of me and begin crossing it." The disciples obey and go to the boat on the lake. Jesus dismisses the crowd and once again retreats to pray. It was evening when he sent his disciples to cross the lake, and he prayed for a long time, almost the whole night.

Meanwhile, the wind stirs up the water. Toward the end of the night, Jesus comes toward them, walking on the water. The sea, this great body of water, is once again, a symbol of sin and death. Why does Jesus walk on the water? Did he perhaps want to demonstrate that he is more capable and physically versatile than others? No. It simply means he has the power to put sin and death under his feet, so much so that he waits for the end of the night because it is toward the end of the night that the resurrection occurs. It is at very early dawn when the women go to the tomb; they find it empty and hear the announcement of the resurrection. Jesus had risen toward the end of the night.

Jesus, walking on the water toward the end of the night, preannounces his resurrection, saying, "I am able to walk over sin and death. I am also the Lord over sin and death."

When the disciples see him, they demonstrate something typical of human beings: we are disposed to believe absurd things rather than surrender to the facts. It is obvious that Jesus is walking on the water, that there is something extraordinary and divine about him, but they are ready instead to say that it is a ghost, to believe something that does not even exist. How many times, just to continue with what we are already thinking, are we willing to believe the irrational and the absurd rather than submit to the evidence of reality? "Take heart, it is I; do not be afraid." The disciples had cried out because they were afraid. Peter, sensing that it is Jesus, says to him, "Lord, if it is you, command me to come to you on the water." Peter's request here is good because he is really saying, "Make me a participant in your life and in your power over these forces."

Jesus says, "Come." The following point is generally overlooked. Getting out of the boat, Peter does start to walk on the water. He too has now walked on water, so good for him for trusting Jesus! Peter was an expert fisherman, so he knew this lake and its dangers well. This is not a body of water in which one can float without knowing how to swim; in this lake one sinks! He obeys Jesus and begins to walk, but then a wind comes up that distracts him from Jesus. As long as he was focused on Jesus and was obeying him and looking at him, he could walk on water, thereby sharing in Jesus's power and resurrection. But then he lets himself get distracted by the wind. Whenever there is a danger or difficulty, what do we do? Peter begins to sink. That is also how spiritual life works. When we pay more attention to our understanding of situations and obstacles, we distract ourselves from Jesus and are not able to keep moving forward;

sin and death then have the upper hand. However, Peter cries out, "Lord, save me!!" This is the really great cry that we ought to address to the Lord. First, calling him Lord, we should say, "You are my God and you are my savior; only you can accomplish this." Secondly, we should say, "Save me in my weakness," which is similar to the cry of the good thief on the cross when he says, "Remember me" (Luke 23:42).

We also learn from Peter the humility of crying out to Jesus, the ability to keep our gaze fixed on him and to know that only if Jesus stretches out his hand can we be saved. Jesus waits for us to cry out to him this way.

Then Jesus reproves Peter: "You of little faith, why did you doubt?" We could think, "Poor Peter. He is walking on the water and a strong wind comes up. It's normal that he was a bit fearful." Yet Jesus reproves him because, although it is true that many things can distract us, he, Jesus, is there and our gaze should be fixed on him. Every time we look away from Jesus, it basically means that we are not trusting him very much, that we are not so sure he is really taking care of us.

They had hardly gotten back into the boat when the wind ceased; it was enough that Jesus was there. "Truly you are the Son of God." We too, after crossing over Lake Tiberias, hope to be able to say not only with our lips and minds but also with our hearts, our wills, our affections, and our emotions, "You are the Son of God." We can choose to fix our gaze on him and not let ourselves become too disturbed by the wind and waves that life will make us experience again, once we return home.

PERSONAL REFLECTION

I fix my gaze on Jesus. I see him victorious over sin and death and wanting me to participate in his victory, so I ask myself:

1. In the various circumstances of my life and in the history of humanity, do I know how to discern the presence of God and his providence?

2. When I feel that God is absent, do I rebel and protest, or do I seek him more fervently?

3. In dangers and difficulties, do I have the humility to cry out to the Lord, "Save me"? Do I believe he is the only one who can save my life?

4. Do I let myself be taught by reality and truth, or am I stubbornly attached to my ideological viewpoints?

PRAYER

I praise you, O Lord, for the power of your word;
I praise you for the victory of your resurrection;
I praise you for the faithfulness of your friendship.

I bless you, Lord,
for the hard work of growing in faith;
I bless you for the waiting that increases my desire for you;
I bless you because
you always hear my cry for help.

Heal the eyes of my faith, Lord;
heal my unbelief;
heal the wounds of sin.

Teach me to recognize your presence, Lord;
teach me to keep my gaze fixed on you;
teach me to abandon myself to you.

7

THE CHURCH OF SAINT ANNE

The Healing of the Paralytic at the Pool

FROM THE GOSPEL ACCORDING TO JOHN (5:1-18)

After this there was a festival of the Jews, and Jesus went up to Jerusalem. Now in Jerusalem by the Sheep Gate there is a pool, called in Hebrew Beth-zatha, which has five porticoes. In these lay many invalids—blind, lame, and paralyzed. One man was there who had been ill for thirty-eight years.

When Jesus saw him lying there and knew that he had been there a long time, he said to him, "Do you want to be made well?" The sick man answered him, "Sir, I have no one to put me into the pool when the water is stirred up; and while I am making my way, someone else steps down ahead of me." Jesus said to him, "Stand up, take your mat and walk." At once the man was made well, and he took up his mat and began to walk.

Now that day was a sabbath. So the Jews said to the man who had been cured, "It is the sabbath; it is not lawful for you to carry your mat." But he answered them, "The man who made me well said to me, 'Take up your mat and walk.'" They asked him, "Who is the man who said to you, 'Take it up and walk'?" Now the man who had been healed did not know who it was, for Jesus had disappeared in the crowd that was there.

Later Jesus found him in the temple and said to him, "See, you have been made well! Do not sin anymore, so that nothing worse happens to you." The man went away and told the Jews that it was Jesus who had made him well. Therefore the Jews started persecuting Jesus, because he was doing such things on the sabbath. But Jesus answered them, "My Father is still working, and I also am working." For this reason the Jews were seeking all the more to kill him, because he was not only breaking the sabbath, but was also calling God his own Father, thereby making himself equal to God.

MEDITATION

The healing of the paralytic at the pool of Beth-zatha (also called Bethesda) is another one of the great signs that John the Evangelist inserts into his Gospel in preparation for the event of the resurrection.

There is a man there, stretched out on his mat, who has been sick for thirty-eight years. The Gospel writer tells us that Jesus passes by and sees him, and just seeing the man moves Jesus; it moves him to compassion, so much so that he approaches him and asks him a question.

It is always valuable to emphasize this constant trait: When Jesus sees, he is moved by compassion and intervenes. This is why it is worthwhile to be in Jesus's presence. We should never be afraid of coming before him in prayer and adoration. It is good to create the conditions for ourselves and for others to be under his gaze. He sees, and in seeing he intervenes according to what is truly good for the person under his gaze.

He sees a man who has been ill for thirty-eight years. He approaches him and asks, "Do you want to be made well?"

The question is not superfluous or trivial; it is instead very much to the point. The man does not say yes or no but says, "I have no one to put me into the pool when the water is stirred up."

This reveals a psychological and spiritual dynamic that is so often present in our lives: the idea of healing frightens us; the idea of leaving behind our problems terrifies us a bit. The thought of leaving our spiritual captivity and our stagnation makes us uneasy. Why? Because we are already familiar with being sick; we are familiar with the problematic situations between men and women; and perhaps we are somewhat fine with all of it. Having illnesses, difficulties, and problems becomes our mode of relating to others and of conversing with them. This can happen because, through our efforts, we are sure of being able to move at least one person. We think that at least one person will notice us, even if only to say, "Oh, poor you!" Sometimes the idea of well-being and having energy scares us because it might mean, "Now I have to fend for myself. There is no one to take care of me." Our complaining, our feeling bad, at times becomes our means of communicating.

This happens in spiritual life as well. Conversion costs us some effort; the decision to convert involves a radical change of life and facing a dimension of existence that we are unfamiliar with (and the unknown causes us fear). So we may prefer to feel sorry for ourselves, to complain about our problems and pains. In the end, we do not convert and we do not change our lives.

We should note that this man says he has no one to help him. If he has been sick and paralyzed for thirty-eight years, someone must be giving him some day-to-day help, so it is not literally true that he had no one. Perhaps he meant that no one was there at the precise time to lower him into the pool. Although in this instance he is responding this way to someone who spontaneously asked him, "Do you want to be made well?" He has someone right there with him, so not why take advantage of the occasion? Now we see that Jesus's question is not trivial; it is precisely accurate. It is as if Jesus were saying, "Is it really true that you want to be healed? Do you want to be saved? Do you want to become a person capable of loving, of having relationships with others, of living your life to its full extent?"

It is the question that we need to let Jesus ask us here today. Let us allow ourselves to be asked, "But you, do *you* want to be healed?" That can be a question we bring with us as we move forward on our path of salvation. The Way of the Cross can be the occasion for us to respond, "Yes, Lord, save me."

Jesus then heals the paralytic, telling him, "Take your mat and go home." In other words, "Take charge of your life and live like a mature and responsible human being. Enough of this life in which you have always been served! It is up to you now to take hold of your life and begin to live responsibly. Get busy!"

PERSONAL REFLECTION

I see Jesus going by the paralytic and he is moved with compassion. I listen to his question and the dialogue that ensues, and I ask myself:

1. Do I come into Jesus's presence? How? When?
2. Do I also encourage the people who are dear to me or who have been entrusted to me to encounter him?
3. Am I focused on myself and my problems? Do I often complain? Do I demand the attention of others?
4. Do I know how to come out of myself and be attentive to whoever is in need or in trouble?
5. Do I really want the Lord to bend over me to heal me and save me?
6. Am I open to understand the new life that Jesus is ready to give me?

PRAYER

How comforting your gaze is, Lord!
It is a unique gaze, different from the gaze of others.
It is a free and freeing gaze.
It is a gaze full of compassion and tenderness.

How authentic your gaze is, Lord!
Under your gaze I am known by you.
Under your gaze all excuses fall away.
Under your gaze the future opens up.

How powerful your gaze is, Lord!
Your eyes penetrate the depths of my heart.
Your eyes reveal your heart to me.
Your eyes heal my eyes.

Save me, Lord!
From my prison.
From my paralysis.
From my inability to love.

8
·······

MOUNT TABOR
The Transfiguration

FROM THE GOSPEL ACCORDING TO LUKE (9:28-36)

Now about eight days after these sayings Jesus took with him Peter and John and James, and went up on the mountain to pray. And while he was praying, the appearance of his face changed, and his clothes became dazzling white. Suddenly they saw two men, Moses and Elijah, talking to him. They appeared in glory and were speaking of his departure, which he was about to accomplish at Jerusalem.

Now Peter and his companions were weighed down with sleep; but since they had stayed awake, they saw his glory and the two men who stood with him. Just as they were leaving him, Peter said to Jesus, "Master, it is good for us to be here; let us make three dwellings, one for you, one for Moses, and one for Elijah"—not knowing what he said.

While he was saying this, a cloud came and overshadowed them; and they were terrified as they entered the cloud. Then from the cloud came a voice that said, "This is my Son, my Chosen; listen to him!" When the voice had spoken, Jesus was found alone. And they kept silent and in those days told no one any of the things they had seen.

MEDITATION

Jesus and his disciples are traveling. A few days earlier at Caesarea Philippi, Jesus had done a kind of survey. He asked his friends, "I have been preaching and performing miracles for a while now, so what do people think of me? You are with the people and hear what they say when I preach and do my works. What do they think of me?" The disciples' answers were all complimentary and noble: "Some say you are Elijah or one of the prophets." But Jesus presses them further:

"You who are my disciples, who are with me twenty-four hours a day, to whom I have confided the secrets of my heart, who have a special intimacy with me, and who have not been distant observers like the others, who do you say that I am?"

Peter as the spokesman for the others responds, "You are the Messiah, the Son of the living God" (Matthew 16:1). Jesus immediately comments on this: "Peter, that is indeed the truth. However, you did not intuit that on your own, and your flesh did not tell you that. This revelation does not come from human intuition but from the Holy Spirit who was moving in you. It is the Father through the Spirit who has told you this." Jesus seems to want to add, "Listen, it is true that I am the Son of God, the Messiah, but I have a unique way of interpreting my status. I am going to Jerusalem now where I will soon be unjustly condemned and crucified, and I will rise up on the third day."

This is extremely scandalous! How is it possible for the Son of God to die? How is it that the Son of God could fail? It is not possible! This is unacceptable for anyone who thinks philosophically and even more so for someone who knows the Jewish Scriptures. God, by definition, cannot die; therefore, the idea that the Messiah could fail is an unthinkable concept. And yet, Jesus insists, "All that I have accomplished so far and my demonstration of truly being the Son of God will undergo what looks like failure and scandal in people's eyes. But I will demonstrate God's power and wisdom in Jerusalem."

The disciples struggle to understand. The Gospels recount honestly that Peter dared to take Jesus aside and admonish him: "Look, Jesus, in my opinion you are very mistaken," and he attempts to instruct Jesus about how things should go.

What does Jesus answer? "Peter, get behind me; it is not your place to stand before me to instruct me; you need to get behind me like a faithful disciple who learns and follows." Nevertheless, Jesus, who knows his disciples well (and knows us too) is merciful. He knows this truth is really difficult to understand because it involves a scandal, so he chooses to do something merciful. He takes three privileged witnesses (who will also be with him at Gethsemane and in other salient moments of his life): Peter, on whom he will found the Church, and the pair of brothers, James and John, who will have specific roles later in the history of the Church.

Jesus goes up this mountain with them. The extraordinary event that we call the Transfiguration occurs here. This word is a bit strange because it literally describes switching from one figure to another, a metamorphosis, a change in visual appearance.

The Gospel writers struggle to describe this event because it does not belong to the human sphere. We are able to describe things that are typically human because we have the appropriate categories and words, but we stutter in trying to communicate the things of God. We need to invent new words that attempt to say at least something, even if we do not succeed in saying everything: "It was Jesus, but they were seeing him in a different way."

It is not easy to recount an experience of God, but it is necessary to delve into this a bit. We could say that for an instant, Jesus, on the Mount of Transfiguration, opened a window into the mystery of God. The disciples were able to see heaven in advance and experience what our inheritance will be for all eternity—to see the mystery of God just as it is. We can intuit the joy and the sense of fullness they felt. This is perhaps why Peter says, "Let us remain here." That is very understandable. Peter had grasped the essence: This is the truth of things, their fullness; this is our destination point. The problem is that Peter wanted to skip all the necessary prerequisites to get there. He had forgotten that Jesus had to go to Jerusalem first and endure his Passion. We could say that Jesus wanted to open this window to heaven and show the final outcome ahead of time in order to give his disciples the strength to bear the events that would be transpiring.

Luke narrates this event within a specific context: Jesus takes Peter, James, and John with him to go up the mountain to pray. This is a typical, ongoing theme in Luke's Gospel because he often emphasizes Jesus's prayer. The Transfiguration is an occasion set in the context of prayer. The Transfiguration is what the disciples witness as they are praying, but we too can experience that in prayer because prayer is an experience of heaven. Pope Benedict XVI taught us that the liturgy, the prayer of the Church, is the space in which heaven and earth meet (General Audience, October 3, 2012). Heaven suddenly erupts onto the earth, and the mystery of God inhabits the mystery of human beings; it touches them and transforms them.

Every time we celebrate Mass the space-time categories are superseded. At Mass we discover that the present moment is also an eternal moment— the moment in which God and human beings meet.

The Transfiguration represents a category of events that occur throughout all of Jesus's life. It is, of course, primarily a specific, identifiable event narrated by all three Synoptic Gospels. At the same time, the idea of transfiguration is something that characterizes his whole existence. Jesus did, in fact, manifest himself in different ways. Isn't the Incarnation also a transfiguration? The Son of God takes on human form by being incarnated. Isn't the Passion of Christ also a kind of transfiguration, and actually even a *disfiguration*? The prophet Isaiah says that he no longer had any appearance or comeliness that would attract us, almost as though he no longer looked human (see Isaiah 53:2). Nevertheless, this Son of God on the cross, the very one who is the sacrificed lamb, is still Jesus, even if he is in another form. Isn't the Eucharist also a transfiguration? It is Jesus himself, but now under the species of bread and wine! How urgent it is today for us to remember that Jesus is really present in the Eucharist!

This event also teaches us to be more discerning in discovering the presence of Jesus in our lives. In the life of a believer there are moments in which he or she feels the need to cry out, "But Lord, where are you?" Perhaps this is because we have in mind only one image of Jesus and, unfortunately, that image is not the one he is offering us of himself right then. At those times we are unable to recognize him as being present. We need to learn instead to discover his presence in the new form in which he desires to manifest himself. And what is the surest way to learn to recognize him? Once again, it is prayer, prayer nourished by God's word because God's word is the truth that sets us free from the pitfalls of our opinions—especially when those opinions sometimes become transformed into ideologies. At times we have an "ideological" image of Jesus. We construct our own Jesus and become attached to that image, and if we do not see him in that specific way, we end up thinking he is absent, and that absence is his fault!

Jesus brings his disciples up Mount Tabor at a serious point in their friendship. They have just learned that he is going to Jerusalem to be killed. This is a difficult time for them, so out of love he shows them heaven in advance.

We have gone up the mountain, starting from the Plain of Esdraelon, and as we looked around during our ascent, we have seen circular and rectangular fields and some villages on the horizon that we could not see before. Little by little as we ascend, we get a different perspective, and at the top we see things again in a new way as each thing takes on its real dimension in proportion to the entire landscape.

Prayer in the life of a Christian has exactly the same function. It takes us away from daily life, which is the plain we start from—often marked by triviality, monotony, and routine—and lifts us up to have a different perspective. When life seems to crush us with problems, challenges, suffering, failures, wounds, and betrayals, prayer opens up the horizon for us and helps us assess each single thing more accurately and move forward. Prayer is a personal (or communal) encounter through which we take on a new perspective about our lives, a perspective from God's point of view.

However, we also need to hear Jesus's invitation to "come back down to the valley." Having been enriched by our experience, we can return to new valleys with the consoling certainty of the final outcome and with the ability to interpret struggles, challenges, failures, and betrayals in light of the experience God has just given us and the inheritance he has prepared for us.

The biggest anxiety a person can have is not to understand the meaning of what is happening. If people learn how to draw the meaning of life from Jesus's Passion, then facing the extraordinary drama of daily life takes on a new significance. Here on Tabor we can ask the Lord for the grace of looking at life from *the perspective of eternity*, not in order to avoid real life but to engage in it in the most authentic and real way.

Personal Reflection

I let Jesus "take me with him" and lead me up the mountain to contemplate the mystery of his divinity. I ask the Holy Spirit to make my gaze be discerning and contemplative so that I may recognize the beauty of God in the transfigured flesh of Jesus.

I look at Jesus and I ask myself:

1. In the course of daily events, do I know how to find space for prayer that will give me a different, accurate perspective for understanding life? For understanding past history?

2. Do I willingly make an effort to "climb up higher," to overcome being captive to my opinions and passions and discover the challenging but liberating force of truth?

3. Do pain, suffering, and anxiety take away my hope, or do I learn to deal with these things from a perspective and a faith that come from the Passover?

4. Do I desire heaven, holiness, and perfect communion with the Lord?

5. Does my encounter with the Lord in the sacraments of the Church transfigure, and thus transform, my life.

PRAYER

The beauty of your face, Lord,
draws my gaze.
The consolation of your victory
gives me strength for my life.
The certainty of eternal life
fills my days with joy.

Heal my eyes, O Lord,
and make me able to recognize you as present and alive.
Capture my gaze
and fix it on the mystery of your Beauty.
Make my vision clear,
and guide my heart to love the truth.

Convert my thoughts, O Lord,
through hearing your voice.
Transform my choices and actions
by the power of your Holy Spirit.
Transform my life to resemble yours
through the power of your love.

9

JERICHO

The Conversion of Zacchaeus

He entered Jericho and was passing through it. A man was there named Zacchaeus; he was a chief tax collector and was rich. He was trying to see who Jesus was, but on account of the crowd he could not, because he was short in stature. So he ran ahead and climbed a sycamore tree to see him, because he was going to pass that way.

When Jesus came to the place, he looked up and said to him, "Zacchaeus, hurry and come down; for I must stay at your house today." So he hurried down and was happy to welcome him. All who saw it began to grumble and said, "He has gone to be the guest of one who is a sinner."

Zacchaeus stood there and said to the Lord, "Look, half of my possessions, Lord, I will give to the poor; and if I have defrauded anyone of anything, I will pay back four times as much."

Then Jesus said to him, "Today salvation has come to this house, because he too is a son of Abraham. For the Son of Man came to seek out and to save the lost."

We can also read and meditate on the passage about the healing of the blind man on the roadside outside Jericho in Luke 18:35-43.

MEDITATION

Jesus enters Jericho. Going through Jericho is almost obligatory for someone going up to Jerusalem when coming from the north and along the Jordan river. Having entered Jericho, he goes through the city. This is a very important fact. When Jesus enters Jericho—a symbolic city because it is the oldest city on earth—he is thereby entering the community of humanity, in which people have banded together. Jesus goes through the city not simply to go through it but to become familiar with it; he wants to enter it and participate in it.

A man called Zacchaeus, the chief tax-collector and a rich man, was trying to see who Jesus was. Who is Zacchaeus? He has two characteristics that make him a person humanly past redemption. First, he is the chief of tax-collectors, the group of people who chose to serve a foreign invader to collect taxes and thus deny God's primacy. Second, he is rich. A few verses earlier in Luke's Gospel, Jesus had said how hard it is for a rich person to enter the Kingdom of Heaven. If we analyze the life of this man from the pastoral point of view, we could say he is a hopeless case. He is one of those people everyone speaks about dejectedly as they shrug their shoulders: "There's nothing more we can do; he is lost." And yet his name is Zacchaeus, a name that some authors translate from Hebrew in two ways: "the clean one" and "the one God remembers." His name apparently contradicts his situation completely. He is someone about whom all the others would say, "He is so unclean that there is nothing more we can do for him; he cannot pray and cannot be saved." And yet he is called "the one God remembers."

Zacchaeus wanted to see who Jesus was. We do not know if this was a pure and genuine desire or only an expression of his curiosity and interest. Nevertheless, Zacchaeus had in fact a desire to see who Jesus was. This brings us to a very precise reflection: the desire for God is one of the things written on people's hearts that cannot be totally suppressed. Even for someone who is humanly and pastorally the most desperate or incurable, there is a wound in the depth of a person's heart that cries out with longing for God and cannot be healed except through an encounter with God himself. It is, therefore, never possible to affirm that there is nothing more that can be done for someone even if it is at the last moment of life.

There were two obstacles to Zacchaeus seeing Jesus: He was short and there was a large crowd. One obstacle was personal, his height, and the second was outside of himself. Very often we also meet these kinds of obstacles in meeting with the Lord. At times the obstacles are outside of us. For example, we enter a church because we have a deep desire to pray, but people next to us are talking, praying in loud voices, or making some kind of noise that prevents us from recollecting ourselves. At other times we are distracted by the things that surround us. We want to focus our thoughts and desires on God, but then we open a newspaper or turn on the TV, and we hear what is happening around us in the work world, or perhaps in our family, and we are aware that everything is leading us in the opposite direction. We have the feeling that things in our daily lives are trying to take away from our desire for God. We have a real propensity to blame all the external causes and condemn them because we believe they are blocking us from encountering the Lord. We do not remember, though, that there may also be an obstacle linked to us personally.

The Gospel says Zacchaeus was a small man, which describes his stature. For us at times, perhaps what is small is our will, our determination or perseverance in seeking the Lord or being in his presence and our attempt to overcome obstacles.

Zacchaeus, an enterprising and quick-witted man, understands it would be good if he met Jesus; he is doomed, a lost person, but he has heard talk about that man. All the caravans that were going through Jericho were bringing a lot of news, especially about Galilee, and would certainly have brought reports about the miracles Jesus had performed (the healing of the paralytic, the multiplication of loaves, the exorcism in the synagogue in Capernaum) and his sermon on the mount. Zacchaeus was curious, fascinated, and interested, so he devises a solution. He climbs the sycamore, allowing him to overcome the obstacles of the crowd and his height. Although he wanted to see Jesus, he was probably asking himself if he would succeed. Just at that moment, Jesus stops under the sycamore.

It is true that we want to encounter Jesus, and it is true that Jesus let himself be encountered, but in the light of this Gospel passage it is clearly more the case that Jesus was going in search of Zacchaeus. Zacchaeus was moving toward Jesus precisely because Jesus himself was already searching for him.

Having come to the sycamore, Jesus calls Zacchaeus by name. It is wonderful and inspiring to hear the revelation in that name: "You are the one God has remembered; I am the presence of God who has remembered you and have come to find you. Come down now because today I need to stay at your house." The verb *need* does not point to a physical need for shelter or rest but expresses a will to save. Jesus is the Word of God himself that we met in Nazareth, who was incarnated in Mary's womb so that God could finally join himself to human beings. Walking through the streets of Israel, Jesus finally arrives in Jericho to seek a man, and he meets him to go home with him.

"I need to stay at your house; I have a great desire to stay at your house." Zacchaeus comes down full of joy. This man who is probably saddened by life, anguished, and upset, welcomes Jesus into his home. The Gospel does not focus on what is happening during the meal but on what is happening outside. The people are scandalized. "Wait a minute. They told us this Jesus was a prophet, but doesn't he know the kind of person he is with? Doesn't he know that by entering the house of this unclean man he becomes unclean himself? How can he be on his way to go up to Jerusalem?" They begin to murmur, which in biblical language means "to lack faith." They lack faith in Jesus. What are the passersby, the citizens of Jericho, doing? In the very city whose walls miraculously crumbled when the people of Israel entered it, the people now erect a wall with their lack of faith that keeps them separated from Jesus.

The Gospel refers to the specific result of this encounter: the conversion of Zacchaeus. While the other citizens of Jericho are "building" a wall of separation from Jesus, the walls that held Zacchaeus's heart as a prisoner crumble at Jesus's word, just like the walls did at the sound of the ancient trumpets. Finally Zacchaeus's heart becomes a beating heart and turns to love. He makes some extraordinary decisions: He will give half of his wealth to the poor and use the other half to restore fourfold whatever he stole from others.

Two significant criteria emerge here that can never be split up: Zacchaeus not only gives to the poor, but he also performs an act of justice. Charity and justice should always go together. He could have given everything to the poor, but this act of charity would not have been genuine if he did not also restore what he had stolen, if he did not act justly. And if he had done only a work of justice in restituting fourfold and had not given to the poor, he would have been only a just man but not a man who had encountered the Lord. Jesus brings about justice through charity and mercy because justice and charity should always go together. Zacchaeus announces this decision when he is standing up, that is, in the position of someone who is raised up. He encountered Jesus and he has risen up to become a new man. The entrance of Jesus into his life is truly a sign that God remembered him, but it is also the occasion of his purification. Finally his name has become true.

"Today salvation has come to this house." Jesus, salvation, entered that house because Zacchaeus was also a son of Abraham. The condition for accessing salvation is not in fact primarily moral—being good or not good—but being a son of Abraham, a man or woman of faith, because Abraham is the father of all believers. Moral choices arise, then, from faith.

"The Son of Man has come to seek out and save the lost." This statement is almost a concise anthropological treatise. What does Jesus think of human beings? People without God are lost, but those who encounter God are saved.

Jericho has certain characteristics that make it unique: It is the most ancient city on earth; it is the city constructed at the lowest point of the earth; it is the largest city built in an oasis. Why would the encounter with

Zacchaeus happen exactly here? Obviously because Zacchaeus was living here and the Lord comes to seek us where we are. But let's speculate allegorically. It would be interesting to think that Jesus, in meeting Zacchaeus here, has encountered Adam, the man he was so passionately seeking, and so Jericho would be the most suitable setting. When Jesus encounters a person there is no past sin, in life or in history, that cannot be forgiven. When Jesus enters a person's life; there is no baseness to which a person has lowered himself or herself (we are at the lowest point of the earth) that cannot be transformed into the heights of friendship with him. When Jesus touches a person, there is no life that had become a desert through the tragedy of sin that cannot be transformed into an oasis full of fruit. These would be three allegorical applications.

PERSONAL REFLECTION

I see Zacchaeus wanting to meet Jesus, and I see Jesus who is looking for Zacchaeus. I see them meet, and I listen to their words, and I ask myself:

1. Do I want to see Jesus?

2. Do I feel the pain of my distance from him because of my sin?

3. Do I devise all possible practical solutions to overcome the obstacles that prevent my encounter with him?

4. Does Jesus's mercy toward sinners scandalize me? Do I imitate him in his capacity to forgive?

5. Does my encounter with Jesus transform me into a just and charitable person?

6. Am I satisfied with doing some good things that placate my conscience, or do I also seek to do justice? Do I limit myself to a dispassionate observance of the law, or do I imitate the love of Jesus who made his life a total gift without reservations?

7. Do I joyfully and enthusiastically proclaim the Gospel to my brothers and sisters, knowing that the full truth about human beings is only found in communion with God?

PRAYER

> Seek me, Lord,
> and teach me to seek you.
>
> Find me, Lord,
> and give me the joy of finding you.
>
> Enter into my house, Lord,
> and cause me to dwell in your presence.
>
> Touch my heart, Lord,
> and make me able to love.

IO
. . . .

BETHANY

Mary, Martha, and Lazarus

From the Gospel according to Luke (10:38-42)

Now as they went on their way, he entered a certain village, where a woman named Martha welcomed him into her home. She had a sister named Mary, who sat at the Lord's feet and listened to what he was saying. But Martha was distracted by her many tasks; so she came to him and asked, "Lord, do you not care that my sister has left me to do all the work by myself? Tell her then to help me." But the Lord answered her, "Martha, Martha, you are worried and distracted by many things; there is need of only one thing. Mary has chosen the better part, which will not be taken away from her."

From the Gospel according to John (12:1-8)

Six days before the Passover Jesus came to Bethany, the home of Lazarus, whom he had raised from the dead. There they gave a dinner for him. Martha served, and Lazarus was one of those at the table with him. Mary took a pound of costly perfume made of pure nard, anointed Jesus' feet, and wiped them with her hair. The house was filled with the fragrance of the perfume. But Judas Iscariot, one of his disciples (the one who was about to betray him), said, "Why was this perfume not sold for three hundred denarii and the money given to the poor?" (He said this not because he cared about the poor, but because he was a thief; he kept the common purse and used to steal what was put into it.) Jesus said, "Leave her alone. She bought it so that she might keep it for the day of my burial. You always have the poor with you, but you do not always have me."

Meditation

Jesus is welcomed into the home of Martha, Mary, and Lazarus by Martha who, the Gospel says, is serving him. Mary is sitting at his feet to listen to him. We have a Gospel scene that is easy to picture in our minds. Martha would have prepared a basin of water for Jesus (to refresh himself and wash his face and feet) and offered him orange or grapefruit juice. In line with the wonderful customs of Middle Eastern hospitality, she is certainly hard at work to make Jesus feel comfortable in her home. Mary is instead seated at his feet to listen to him. At a certain point Martha reproaches Jesus, "Don't you care? Don't you realize Mary is only listening to you and is not helping me out at all? Say something to her." Martha is attempting to instruct Jesus about what he should say to Mary. Jesus answers her with his very famous statement, "Martha, Martha, you are worried and distracted by many things; there is need of only one thing. Mary has chosen the better part, which will not be taken away from her." Let's examine this sentence carefully.

Jesus calls Martha by her name and does so twice, as if to say, "I have something very important to tell you."

"You are worried and distracted by many things." There are three characteristics that define Martha's personality: *you are worried, you are distracted, many things.* Jesus is inviting her to have a triple conversion, to move away from having these three attitudes to having three new ones.

You are worried: What does it mean to be worried? It means filling one's life with many things to chase after and to be anxious about.

You are distracted. What is a distraction or preoccupation? It is a thought that occupies my mind and my faculties before a thing happens. I'm aware of the effort I will need to expend when it does happen, but it is also robbing my energy and is not allowing me to live well in the present. If I am not living well in the present, then I will not succeed in having my life and energy ready to face the issue that is already bothering me, so I will face it in a less effective way.

Many things. There are so many preoccupations and reasons for worry that divide my attention. They divide my heart and my life.

What does Jesus ask Martha and, through Martha, each one of us? To choose the better part is primarily to go from agitation to peace. Mary is at Jesus's feet; she is not anxious; she is calm; she is not moving around. He is asking us to go from being preoccupied to being attentive. While Martha is preoccupied with many things Mary is paying attention to Jesus. Martha is attending to many things while Mary is attentive to the one thing that is needed, which is to learn from Jesus.

In brief, Jesus is asking us to move from worry to calm, from distraction to attention, from many things to the one thing that is needed.

In Martha's eyes, Mary had made herself comfortable and was not demonstrating an appropriate welcome to Jesus. He instead emphasizes that it was precisely Mary who had welcomed him because she had offered him the "room" of her heart by listening and being open to his instruction.

This does not mean that Jesus did not appreciate Martha's service or that activity is not important in our lives. Too often Martha and Mary are set in opposition to each other as if one were the negation of the other. This can annoy those who are busy all day long since it makes it seem that their work is not dignified. This is not the case, since Martha is also recognized as a saint. Jesus instead wants to teach his disciples that the core of everything is listening, the inner welcome of Jesus. If we have a profound acceptance of this in our hearts and consciences, all our actions can be authentic without worry and distraction. Mary was able to sit at Jesus's feet and receive him into her heart, to let herself be shaped by his word. She understood in a prophetic and intuitive way what was going to happen to Jesus. John's Gospel tells us that six days before Passover, Jesus went to Bethany to the home of Martha, Mary, and Lazarus where they had prepared a meal for him and his disciples. During the meal, Mary leaves the table and gets an alabaster vase containing the ointment used for the burial of the dead. She pours this ointment on Jesus's body, anointing it. (A parallel Gospel passage, Mark 14:3, emphasizes that the alabaster jar was broken so that all the perfume came forth!) Her action astounds everybody because it was an uncommon gesture that was done only for a dead body and not for a living person. Judas protests against her action and refuses to accept this waste. "Why? We could have sold it for 300 denarii and given it to the poor." But Jesus reproaches Judas, saying, "You always have the poor with you, but you do not always have me. Let her do it because she is doing it in preparation for my burial. Moreover, I tell you that wherever the Gospel will be proclaimed what she has done will be told in memory of her." We all do, in fact, know about her gesture.

Mary intuited that this was the last, definitive, decisive time Jesus would be at her home, and she performed an act that imitated Jesus's act on the cross. She performs an act that seems to be wasteful, but it has the particular quality of representing totality, exactly what Jesus is about to do on the cross.

St. Thomas Aquinas's beautiful hymn of adoration of the Eucharist, "*Adoro Te Devote*," at a certain point says, "…clean me with Your blood, / One drop of which can free / the entire world of all its sins." Jesus performs this total gift of himself, which could have seemed like a waste. Mary is celebrating in advance this total gift of love by using all the oil for this anointing, an action that seems wasteful in the eyes of Judas, the treasurer.

There are two reactions to Jesus who is going up to Jerusalem and who is, at this moment, love itself who is going to make a gift of himself: that of Mary, who imitates the dynamic of that gift in being freely and completely given, and the opposite one of Judas, who instead behaves selfishly like a thief who wants to steal the money for himself. These are experiences that we, too, can have in our lives at times.

Every time we have an opportunity to experience love, in the many forms in which it can occur, we should always ask ourselves if we are imitating love in its dynamic of total self-gift or if we are instead acting like thieves, acting selfishly, and therefore killing love itself.

PERSONAL REFLECTION

I watch Jesus in that home in Bethany. I see the friendship and the events of daily life that are occurring there. And I ask myself:

1. What upsets me? What preoccupations absorb all my energy? What threatens to fragment my life by compromising my serenity?
2. In what or in whom do I find the unifying center that gives meaning and peace to my daily life?
3. Do I know how to defend myself from worries and anxieties?
4. How do I live out my relationships? By being selfish or by making my life a free gift of love?
5. Is my attitude more like Martha's or Mary's? More like Judas's or Mary's?
6. What attitudes do I concretely need to change to become more like Jesus?

PRAYER

Lord Jesus, your presence
fills life with joy,
calms our hearts,
frees us from anxiety.

Lord Jesus, your friendship
brings savor to our lives,
opens us up to hope,
consoles us in our sorrow.

Lord Jesus, your love
brings us salvation,

converts our hearts,
snatches us from death.

Lord Jesus, the fragrance of your Passover
draws us into your presence,
keeps us in your friendship,
makes us conform to your love.

11

········

DOMINUS FLEVIT

Jesus Weeps over Jerusalem

FROM THE GOSPEL ACCORDING TO LUKE (19:41-44)

As he came near and saw the city, he wept over it, saying, "If you, even you, had only recognized on this day the things that make for peace! But now they are hidden from your eyes. Indeed, the days will come upon you, when your enemies will set up ramparts around you and surround you, and hem you in on every side. They will crush you to the ground, you and your children within you, and they will not leave within you one stone upon another; because you did not recognize the time of your visitation from God."

FROM THE GOSPEL ACCORDING TO MATTHEW (23:37-39)

"Jerusalem, Jerusalem, the city that kills the prophets and stones those who are sent to it! How often have I desired to gather your children together as a hen gathers her brood under her wings, and you were not willing! See, your house is left to you, desolate. For I tell you, you will not see me again until you say, '*Blessed is the one who comes in the name of the Lord.*'"

MEDITATION

The last time Jesus goes up to Jerusalem, very shortly before being arrested and crucified, he bursts into tears when looking over the city of Jerusalem. The Gospel says, "As he came near and saw the city, he wept over it, saying, "If you, even you, had only recognized on this day the things that make for peace! But now they are hidden from your eyes."

Let us look at Jesus's weeping over Jerusalem and be instructed by it. Jesus looks at the city and weeps. Instinctively we could think that he does so because he knows that in a few days he will suffer and be crucified, so he weeps at the thought of his death. But this is not the case; he is not weeping about his painful suffering and death; he is weeping because his death means that the Chosen People, those who should have received him, have rejected God's love. He was going up to Jerusalem to give himself out of love, but his death will go through a rejection. I believe there is no greater suffering in life than to perceive that one's love is rejected. The great mystics—Francis of Assisi, Teresa of Avila, John of the Cross—in various ways have cried out, "Love is not loved." The real tragedy is the rejection of God's love. The rejection of the love of God fundamentally has a very precise name, which Pope Benedict XVI has alluded to in his encyclical on hope: it is called hell (see *Spe Salvi*, 45). This is exactly what hell is: the refusal by a human being of God's salvific love.

In his letters St. Paul tells us there are two kinds of grief: one that is the consequence of sin and a person's own fault and holy grief that shares the passionate love of God and leads to repentance for one's sins and a desire for salvation.

Let us ask Jesus in this place to teach us about grief.

How many times do we groan and cry, even if the tears are not real, for things that are not very significant in life! It seems that when some good things are taken away from us, or we fail to reach the goals we had set, it is the end of the world for us. It seems we are missing out on life, but often it does not involve anything essential. And yet we do not experience the same suffering when we see that communion with the Lord, for us or for others, is compromised.

The word *passion* has two shades of meaning, both of which are good. Passion is certainly a kind of suffering, a sorrow, but passion is also an inner stirring that can lead us to something else. Jesus demonstrates to us here both aspects of this word: his *passion* of love for the Father and for the salvation of human beings leads him to undergo a *passion* of suffering. Our Christian life should imitate Jesus in this: to be so passionate about God and salvation that we accept the suffering of giving up our goals and projects and what we believe to be right in order to adhere to his will. Jesus taught us that in the Our Father: "May your will be done."

Here we can learn to assess the quality of our suffering for others. Parents, for example, can often suffer because a child is sick, and that is legitimate. They experience pain when a son or daughter causes anxieties because of not finding a job or succeeding in reaching their established goals. Catechists or educators who work hard experience the same thing when they see their service does not seem to achieve the desired results. These are all legitimate instances of suffering in helping to share the struggles of others, but the really great suffering of parents or teachers is to see that a son or daughter or a person entrusted to them does not love the Lord. That is the only suffering that truly deserves tears. Parents or people highly committed to the good of others are disposed to fast, to stay awake entire nights, to go to the ends of the earth for the person they love. Let us ask ourselves, are we disposed to keep vigil, to fast, to do some kind of penance so that the people entrusted to us turn to Jesus Christ to confess their sins and receive the Eucharist?

Through his weeping, Jesus purifies our desires and helps us turn back to what is truly essential.

Let us keep silence with a heartfelt prayer, and let us intercede so we truly desire, for ourselves and others, that all the people we know, and those whom we do not know, are given no rest until they find Jesus, until they rediscover communion with him and let themselves be loved by him. We can unite some of our suffering to that of Jesus, but we should be oriented this way: We are assisting Jesus in undergoing his passion of love and suffering so that all of humanity will welcome his visitation.

Jesus said that in Jerusalem no stone would be left on top of another. Forty years after these words Roman troops razed Jerusalem to the ground and leveled it. Something similar happens in our lives too. Everything we want to build and desire, if it is not in conformity with the Lord's will, will remain a leveled area, foreshadowing the marble slab that will cover our tombs. If instead we desire what Jesus desires and are passionate for him, through him, and with him, then whatever it is will be leveled but that which is essential will remain and remain eternally.

On the Mount of the Beatitudes we hear, "Blessed are those who mourn," those who suffer to the point of tears, because they will be comforted. We said earlier that Jesus was already speaking about himself in that beatitude. He mourned and wept in his passion of love and in his death. But he is smiling now, comforted by his resurrection.

We, too, are called to share his grief in order to enjoy the same comfort forever, through all eternity. Nothing will be able to undercut that consolation.

PERSONAL REFLECTION

I see Jesus weeping over Jerusalem, his city, and I ask myself:

1. Am I able to weep? What is the quality of my grief?
2. What really causes me to suffer?
3. Am I able to share the suffering of others?
4. What do I truly desire deep down?

PRAYER

Lord Jesus,
you love us with a passionate love;
you love us to point of death on the cross;
you suffer for my insensitivity.

Lord Jesus,
train my grief;
train my desire;
train and orient all my faculties toward you.

12
·······

THE CENACLE
The Last Supper

From the Gospel according to Luke (22:7-23)

Then came the day of Unleavened Bread, on which the Passover lamb had to be sacrificed. So Jesus sent Peter and John, saying, "Go and prepare the Passover meal for us that we may eat it." They asked him, "Where do you want us to make preparations for it?" "Listen," he said to them, "when you have entered the city, a man carrying a jar of water will meet you; follow him into the house he enters and say to the owner of the house, 'The teacher asks you, "Where is the guest room, where I may eat the Passover with my disciples?"' He will show you a large room upstairs, already furnished. Make preparations for us there.'" So they went and found everything as he had told them; and they prepared the Passover meal.

When the hour came, he took his place at the table, and the apostles with him. He said to them, "I have eagerly desired to eat this Passover with you before I suffer; for I tell you, I will not eat it until it is fulfilled in the kingdom of God." Then he took a cup, and after giving thanks he said, "Take this and divide it among yourselves; for I tell you that from now on I will not drink of the fruit of the vine until the kingdom of God comes." Then he took a loaf of bread, and when he had given thanks, he broke it and gave it to them, saying, "This is my body, which is given for you. Do this in remembrance of me." And he did the same with the cup after supper, saying, "This cup that is poured out for you is the new covenant in my blood. But see, the one who betrays me is with me, and his hand is on the table. For the Son of Man is going as it has been determined, but woe to that one by whom he is betrayed!" Then they began to ask one another which one of them it could be who would do this.

From the Gospel according to John (20:19-29)

When it was evening on that day, the first day of the week, and the doors of the house where the disciples had met were locked for fear of the Jews, Jesus came and stood among them and said, "Peace be with you." After he said this, he showed them his hands and his side. Then the disciples rejoiced when they saw the Lord. Jesus said to them again, "Peace be with you. As the Father has sent me, so I send you." When he had said this, he breathed on them and said to them, "Receive the Holy Spirit. If you forgive the sins of any, they are forgiven them; if you retain the sins of any, they are retained."

But Thomas (who was called the Twin), one of the twelve, was not with them when Jesus came. So the other disciples told him, "We have seen the Lord." But he said to them, "Unless I see the mark of the nails in his hands, and put my finger in the mark of the nails and my hand in his side, I will not believe."

A week later his disciples were again in the house, and Thomas was with them. Although the doors were shut, Jesus came and stood among them and said, "Peace be with you." Then he said to Thomas, "Put your finger here and see my hands. Reach out your hand and put it in my side. Do not doubt but believe." Thomas answered him, "My Lord and my God!" Jesus said to him, "Have you believed because you have seen me? Blessed are those who have not seen and yet have come to believe."

Meditation

The Cenacle, the room on the second floor spoken of by the Gospel, is one of the most treasured and beautiful places connected to our faith. That is the case even though it causes suffering for us today to know that we cannot pray or celebrate here. For historical reasons of property transfers and at times theft and usurpation, Christian worship is not permanently allowed here. The current walls of this cross-shaped room are thus not exactly the walls of the room Jesus was in. However, we do know that the uninterrupted tradition of the Church has recognized this place in which Jesus was together with his disciples on the last night of his earthly life for what we call the Last Supper.

So many mysteries are concentrated in this place. Let us think about the fact that at least four sacraments were instituted in this place: Eucharist, Holy Orders, Penance, and Confirmation. These sacraments, these four great efficacious signs of grace, instituted in this place indicate the immense value of the Cenacle.

We also remain fascinated by the intimacy of the relationship between Jesus and his disciples. Let us consider the discourses that he delivered here during the Last Supper: the very beautiful image of the vine and branches, which is one of the most concise passages in all of the New Testament; his discourse on brotherly love and loving one another as he loved us; Jesus's great priestly prayer in John 17 in which he prayed, furthermore, that they all might be one. The grand gesture of the foot-washing in John 13 is not simply a sign of humility or of practical service but is the key to interpreting the meaning of Jesus's death and the Eucharist itself. John situates this event right where the other Gospel writers refer to the institution of the Eucharist. John wrote his Gospel for the Christian communities that were already regularly celebrating Sunday Eucharist but were at risk of losing the significance of what they were doing weekly. John seems to be saying, "I am explaining it this way just as the Lord explained it to us on the night he was betrayed." The foot-washing is the symbolic gesture through which Jesus prepared his disciples to think about the mystery of his death and to understand how the Eucharist is the renewal of that same gift of love. "Through my death, which is the gift of my body and blood, I am doing the highest service of life for you that can be done. I wash your life; I save it; I bring it into full communion with the Father." This is why Jesus threatens to exclude Peter from having any part in him if he rejects Jesus's gesture. This is the approach that every disciple of the Lord Jesus should take: mutual service through the gift of one's life for the salvation for brothers and sisters.

We can also listen here to the dialogue between Jesus and his disciples when Jesus reveals the betrayal by Judas and Peter's denial. We can also recall the drama of Judas exiting at night, Peter's desire to remain faithful to the Lord Jesus, but also the clarity with which Jesus unmasks Peter's weakness. At the same time, though, we hear Jesus's consoling and beautiful words to Peter about having prayed for him.

Here we feel protected by Jesus's prayer.

We cannot forget the apparitions of the Risen One. With all the effort in describing the risen body of the Lord, the account seems almost infantile and so simply described: They were in the Cenacle with the doors closed. Jesus comes in—it was he—with the wounds of his passion!

Thinking of Easter night and the event eight days later, let us pause for a moment to consider the extraordinary meeting with Thomas.

Easter night, Jesus appears to his disciples, showing them the wounds in his hands and his side. He breathes the Holy Spirit on them and communicates the gift of peace, the fruit of Easter, but Thomas is not present. And his absence cannot be accidental: Jesus did not wait for his return to the Cenacle but appeared when Thomas had left, perhaps for some urgent task despite all the risks and dangers that entailed.

Jesus appears as risen and alive to his disciples while Thomas is absent, perhaps to make Thomas experience the struggle of believing, of going from unbelief to faith, because that would be instructive for us too. The Fathers of the Church claim that Thomas's unbelief is more useful for us than the faith of the other disciples. Let us try to imagine Thomas's return to the house. Distressed, with his heart in his throat because he has come through the dangers in the city, he finally knocks at the door of the Cenacle. They open up the door and while he is still experiencing fear, he sees the shining faces of the others who tell him, "We have seen the Lord!" That had to be a serious blow. "I went out risking my life for you, and now you are playing a trick on me?" The faces of Peter, John, James, and of the others were definitely shining, intriguing, and that look could not be feigned. Their faces were so beautiful and clear!

It is not difficult to imagine that the disciples had approached Thomas all week long, one by one, to convince him: "We really have seen the Lord! He is risen!" Thomas is significantly surnamed Didymus (Twin) here as though to underscore his interior struggle and the division in his heart. On the one hand, he would have wanted to trust his friends who were recounting such things in such a convincing way; on the other hand, he is unable to believe in an event—the resurrection—that was unheard of, even unimaginable.

We can also think of Mary, who was certainly present in the Cenacle. This mother could not tell Thomas a lie on such a serious topic. And yet Thomas struggles! And he makes a demand with aggressive stipulations: "I want to thrust (literally!) my hand into his side and my finger in the place of the nail holes." A cruel but ingenious request. It was eight days later, in fact, that Jesus, following a significant pattern for our spiritual lives that indicates the recurring role of Sunday for a Christian, appears again in the Cenacle. And this time Thomas is present!

As he appears, Jesus directly addresses the unbelieving disciple and invites him to do exactly what he had demanded. Why did Jesus go along with Thomas's request? Possibly in Jesus's eyes it was not simply a whim on Thomas's part! What is the ingenious part of Thomas's demand? He had understood that if Jesus, the one who gave his life through love, was truly risen and alive, then he and only he deserved total adherence and a commitment of one's life without reservation.

Let us listen to Jesus's words to Thomas: "Do not doubt but believe." It is a word that creates what it says. Just as sometime earlier Jesus had rescued his friend Lazarus from the grave saying, "Come forth," now he seems to be saying to Thomas, "Come forth out of your unbelief and come into faith." This is the word we ask Jesus to speak over our lives, to rescue us from our unbelief. If we are still sinners, if we are often lacking and fail in our friendship with Jesus, it is because we are not yet sufficiently believers; something in our minds, our wills, or our affections is still unbelieving. Let us ask for this grace here in this holy place: "Rescue me, Lord, from my unbelief and bring me to faith." May it be granted to us to unite ourselves to Thomas in asserting, "My Lord and my God!" May the Lord grant us the grace to trust and rely on the proclamation of the Church, which is founded on the testimony and faith of the apostles, including that of Thomas.

This is a place of great grace that holds so many mysteries: The outpouring of the Holy Spirit reaches us, heals us, and makes us disciples of the Lord Jesus.

PERSONAL REFLECTION

I pause over one of the events that transpired in the Cenacle. I examine the actions in it and listen to the words again. I ask myself:

1. Am I able to offer thanks and praise to the Lord who has left us a legacy of all the gifts of grace necessary for us to live as disciples?
2. Do I joyfully and frequently draw from the wellspring of his love?
3. Do I believe in the real presence of Jesus in the Eucharist, the memorial of his Passover?
4. Do I foster the same sentiments Jesus had, especially those on the last night of his life?
5. Do I trust the proclamation of the Church? Is it enough for me to have the testimony of the apostles who experienced the struggle to believe before me and for my sake?

6.   Do I understand what it means to love like Jesus? Do I find ways to obey the new commandment about love?

PRAYER

Lord Jesus,
you eagerly desired
to eat the Passover supper with your disciples.
Place in me the same desire to partake in
your total gift of self to the Father.

Lord Jesus,
You gently took care of your friends
and kept them in the truth.
Help me never separate myself
from your friendship and your safe-keeping.

Lord Jesus,
You overcame Thomas's unbelief
and made the apostles strong and courageous.
Rescue me from unbelief and cause me to say,
"My Lord and my God!"

Lord Jesus,
You have filled the Church
with your peace, your Spirit, and your grace.
Fill my life with your gifts;
dwell in me and lead me to eternal life.

13

GETHSEMANE

The Agony in the Garden

Jesus went out as usual to the Mount of Olives, and his disciples followed him. On reaching the place, he said to them, "Pray that you will not fall into temptation." He withdrew about a stone's throw beyond them, knelt down and prayed, "Father, if you are willing, take this cup from me; yet not my will, but yours be done." An angel from heaven appeared to him and strengthened him. And being in anguish, he prayed more earnestly, and his sweat was like drops of blood falling to the ground. When he rose from prayer and went back to the disciples, he found them asleep, exhausted from sorrow. "Why are you sleeping?" he asked them. "Get up and pray so that you will not fall into temptation."

Meditation

This is the place of Jesus's agony. Isaiah prophetically describes the circumstances of a certain man, and in his description of the suffering servant we can truly recognize Jesus as he is going through his agony.

Let us look at the event that takes place here at night, after Jesus had finished the meal with his disciples. In this garden at the foot of the Mount of Olives called Gethsemane, he goes through his agony. The Greek word *agonia* means "battle." Jesus faces his definitive battle here. At the end of the account of the desert temptations, Luke states, "When the devil had finished every test, he departed from him until an opportune time" (Luke 4:13). This is now the opportune time. Satan is on a rampage now against Jesus because he wants to separate Jesus's human will from the divine will here.

In the ancient Garden of Eden the man and woman were given a command: "You may freely eat of every tree of the garden; but of the tree of the knowledge of good and evil you shall not eat" (Genesis 2:16-17).

Dwelling in that garden meant being admitted to communion with God. That was the original condition of human beings: They could see God face to face and be in communion with him, but they had one single command. They could not put themselves in God's place since he is the one who distinguishes good from evil. Once they were tempted, the man and woman presumed they could make themselves similar to God. The demon's temptation ripped man's will from God's will and a fracture occurred, so heaven was closed. The dramatic consequence of this disobedience involved being chased out of the garden. The man and woman broke friendship with God and self-expelled themselves from communion with God. The whole history of salvation is the great pursuit of love by God to readmit human beings to that communion.

Jesus, the Word of God made flesh by assuming our human nature into his human-divine Person, is called to bring God and human beings back into unity. It is clear that Satan is unleashed and wants to destroy this communion. He did not want Jesus's human will to accept God's will for the salvation of human beings, and Jesus struggled to the point of sweating blood in this garden. If this image can be useful, one of the definitions of Gethsemane—certainly suggestive if perhaps not entirely precise—is "the place of the olive-press." Jesus is pressed in this fight to the point of shedding blood for our salvation. Jesus definitively wins in this garden, demonstrating what he had taught us in the *Our Father*: "Not my will but yours be done" (Luke 22:42). Precisely by obeying the Father, he showed himself to be a profoundly free man; he did not at all consider the human burden, his own interests, and the fear of suffering but considered instead the truth and the true good. Remaining anchored to the truth and the good, he obeyed, and this brought about our salvation.

The disciples who are witnesses of this event are the same as those at the Transfiguration: Peter, James, and John. The Gospel says Jesus arrives at Gethsemane with his disciples but then distances himself a bit. This is a battle that Jesus needs to face by himself. He asks his companions to keep watch with him and to pray not to enter into temptation, but he needs to face this hour in solitude.

The disciples do not hold up; they are not capable of keeping vigil and they fall asleep. But this sleep is certainly not a sign of weariness. In the Cenacle they had just witnessed events that must have electrified them. No one goes to sleep after hearing and seeing the things that had just happened. So what kind of sleep is this? It is a way of escape. Sleep is the thing in life that most resembles death; it can be a way of escape. The disciples do not actually want to see this moment happen, to face this moment. How many ways we find to anesthetize our consciences and our minds, filling our schedules with appointments, filling our minds with noise, burdening ourselves in useless preoccupations with things we do not need, to avoid focusing our hearts, our gaze, our minds, our wills, and our emotions on the one thing that matters! We fear the struggle of facing the reality of daily life that makes us encounter the truth about ourselves, so we seek various subterfuges to avoid having to confront ourselves. Jesus asks us to keep watch with him, to look at reality, to choose the good, to remain anchored to him with our whole being, whatever it costs, because this is the only way to be free and to overcome.

During times of pilgrimage we have the blessing of visiting many places connected to Jesus's life and to meditate on all the fundamental mysteries of his life. Here in the silence of this place, let us try to be together with Jesus. Of course there may have been places that have impressed us more and some texts of the word of God that may have affected us more. However, let us try in this place to say, "I know that a basic struggle awaits; I will be your companion in this hour of your struggle because I know that you will then be my companion in my everyday struggles. Only you can tell me how to do the Father's will in my life, which is the only good path for my life."

Let us unite ourselves to Jesus's suffering and to the weakness of the disciples. Let us ask, through their intercession, that we be allowed to be companions of Jesus; to be united to him and to his struggle; and to share his will so that our human wills will not be separated, divided, or loosed from the good that the Father has for our lives, so that we may come out of the struggle victorious and have our prayers answered.

Mary of Bethany (which is behind this hill) has taught us that only one thing is needed. Jesus repeats to us as well, "Stay here and keep watch." Let us take this moment to obey that command joyfully.

PERSONAL REFLECTION

I watch Jesus as he prays and struggles in the Garden of Olives. I listen to the words he addresses to the Father and to Peter, James, and John. I see the disciples sleeping, and I ask myself:

1. Do I sense any urgency to keep watch and to pray not to fall into temptation?
2. Do I safeguard my communion with God as the most precious good in my life?
3. Do I flee from reality by anesthetizing my conscience and my heart?
4. What part of God's will do I have the hardest time accepting?
5. Am I able to say, "Father, may your will, not mine, be done"?

PRAYER

I see you struggling, O Lord Jesus,

I contemplate your obedience to the Father;

I worship your total abandonment to him;

I am moved by the love that sustains you.

I see you being vulnerable, O Lord Jesus:

you do not fear manifesting your humanity;

you do not hide your cry of sorrow;

you do not flee from the suffering of solitude.

I hear your words, O Lord Jesus:
I contemplate your sovereign freedom;
I adore your filial love;
your joyful sacrifice moves me.

I hear your words, O Lord Jesus;
I discover the cost of truth;
I savor the taste of freedom;
I choose the path of vigilance.

14

THE GROTTO OF
THE ARREST

Judas Betrays Jesus

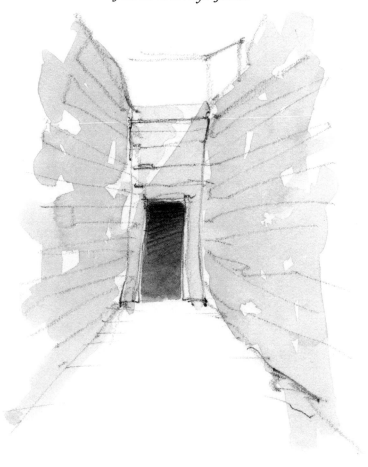

FROM THE GOSPEL ACCORDING TO MARK (14:43-52)

Just as he was speaking, Judas, one of the Twelve, appeared. With him was a crowd armed with swords and clubs, sent from the chief priests, the teachers of the law, and the elders. Now the betrayer had arranged a signal with them: "The one I kiss is the man; arrest him and lead him away under guard." Going at once to Jesus, Judas said, "Rabbi!" and kissed him. The men seized Jesus and arrested him. Then one of those standing near drew his sword and struck the servant of the high priest, cutting off his ear. "Am I leading a rebellion," said Jesus, "that you have come out with swords and clubs to capture me? Every day I was with you, teaching in the temple courts, and you did not arrest me. But the Scriptures must be fulfilled." Then everyone deserted him and fled. A young man, wearing nothing but a linen garment, was following Jesus. When they seized him, He fled naked, leaving his garment behind.

MEDITATION

Let us try to enter Judas's mind. He is standing before the scandal of a Messiah who has decided to be a Messiah through death. Something is not right here.

Judas's betrayal is certainly an enormous betrayal. In the face of the tragedy of this betrayal, let us try to understand—without claiming to understand the mystery of the human heart to its very depths—what could have possibly moved Judas.

In some way it seems as though in handing Jesus over to the Temple priests, Judas was wanting to hand him over to a judge. It is as if Judas were saying to himself, "Let's see if the experts are telling me the truth: Is he really the Messiah or not?"

We know that according to the Jewish way of thinking, death on the cross was actually a death that indicated God's condemnation. If the authorities for the people, the priests, condemn him to this death, it means they do not recognize him as having truly come from God.

This is not a question of diminishing the betrayal. It is still completely horrendous because Judas had known Jesus intimately and had adhered to him. Therefore, he himself could have issued a "judgment" without having to involve the Temple priests. However, we can understand and hypothesize this dynamic: the attempt to subject the Master to the judgment of someone else who had more authority than he did.

The true verdict will be given by God himself in raising Jesus from the dead, and that will be the definitive judgment that demonstrates the unprecedented seriousness of Judas's betrayal.

When Judas arrives, Jesus attempts to reach out to him, calling him "Friend" (Matthew 26:50)—he does not call him by name—"Are you betraying the Son of Man with a kiss?" (Luke 22:48). In other words, "Are you betraying me with the usual sign of love?" He calls Judas "friend" as if to remind him of who he is and to whom he belongs in order to bring him back to a consciousness of his identity: "You are really ruining yourself by selling me out."

They arrest Jesus.

Judas betrays Jesus in this place, and shortly after that Peter denies him.

To deny does not simply mean saying, "I do not know you." Jesus said, "If any want to become my followers, let them deny themselves and take up their cross daily and follow me" (Luke 9:23). The Greek verb for *deny*, *arenomai*, means, "I do not trust this person; I do not consider him the source of my salvation." When people deny themselves to follow Jesus, it is as if they are saying, "I do not delude myself that I am the savior of my life; you, Jesus, are the only Lord of my life."

Jesus asks us to deny ourselves because there cannot be two lords over our lives: One or the other wins out. Peter's denial, then, which was certainly done out of fear of undergoing the same fate as Jesus, risks becoming drastic by no longer acknowledging Jesus as capable of saving his life.

First Judas betrays him, and then Peter denies him. These two behaviors are similar in some ways. The agents of betrayal and denial are two of Jesus's friends, and this alerts us that betrayal and denial can only be done by friends. Enemies will never betray because they are already enemies!

It is good for us to be alerted to this terrible possibility so that we may remain vigilant. We are friends of Jesus, and we are exposed to the risk of betraying him. We cannot delude ourselves into thinking that we will automatically be faithful just because we are his friends. We need to choose to remain faithful and to be vigilant in order not to betray him. If this could happen to Peter—who had already received all possible confidence from Jesus and been pre-selected by him to be the rock upon which he would build his Church—and if Judas—who had experienced Jesus's trust in him and been called by him to the group of twelve and been consigned the group's common purse—could betray him, it means that we, too, are not immune to this risk.

PERSONAL REFLECTION

I see Judas kissing Jesus, and I see Jesus letting him, allowing himself to be arrested. I ask myself:

1. Am I aware of the tragic possibility of being able to betray and deny Jesus? Or do I presume faithfulness on my part?

2. Do I sense the gravity of my sin that actually threatens and affects my friendship with Jesus?

3. Do I let Jesus summon me back to full awareness, awakening in me the joy of being his friend?

4. Whom do I radically trust? Myself or Jesus?

PRAYER

Jesus, you are a faithful friend!
You do not give up on me because of my weakness;
you are not scandalized by my sin;
you do not indulge in retaliation.

Jesus, you are the only savior!
You do not avoid betrayal;
you do not shrink from pain;
you do not flee from solitude and abandonment.

Jesus, you are the Lord!
Forgive my sin,
heal my unfaithfulness,
Keep me in your friendship.

15

ST. PETER IN GALLICANTU

Peter Denies Jesus

From the Gospel according to Luke (22:28-34, 54-62)

"You are those who have stood by me in my trials. And I confer on you a kingdom, just as my Father conferred one on me, so that you may eat and drink at my table in my kingdom and sit on thrones, judging the twelve tribes of Israel. Simon, Simon, Satan has asked to sift all of you as wheat. But I have prayed for you, Simon, that your faith may not fail. And when you have turned back, strengthen your brothers." But he replied, "Lord, I am ready to go with you to prison and to death." Jesus answered, "I tell you, Peter, before the rooster crows today, you will deny three times that you know me." …

Then seizing him, they led him away and took him into the house of the high priest. Peter followed at a distance. And when some there had kindled a fire in the middle of the courtyard and had sat down together, Peter sat down with them. A servant girl saw him seated there in the firelight. She looked closely at him and said, "This man was with him." But he denied it. "Woman, I don't know him," he said. A little later someone else saw him and said, "You also are one of them." "Man, I am not!" Peter replied. About an hour later another asserted, "Certainly this fellow was with him, for he is a Galilean." Peter replied, "Man, I don't know what you're talking about!" Just as he was speaking, the rooster crowed. The Lord turned and looked straight at Peter. Then Peter remembered the word the Lord had spoken to him: "Before the rooster crows today, you will disown me three times." And he went outside and wept bitterly.

Meditation

Jesus announces to Simon his upcoming denial at the Last Supper. Simon, as usual with enthusiasm, said he would follow Jesus right to the end. But

Jesus said to him, "Simon, Simon...before the rooster crows twice today, you will deny that you know me three times." This demonstrates how much the truth needs to have detailed coordinates to help us recognize it. Jesus, almost as though he were a kind of naval battleship, thus gives coordinates linked to time and particular characteristics: There will be two times the cock crows and three denials, so when you get there, you will recognize what happened. Since Peter was presuming he could remain faithful on his own despite everything, Jesus gives him some criteria to be aware of his weakness, even calling him not Peter but Simon—his ordinary name prior to the Lord's renaming of him. It is as though Jesus were saying, "Look, you are not yet Peter and not yet a rock." It would have been as if he had said, "*Sandman, Sandman,...*nothing can be built on you as you are now; you still need to become a rock, so don't count on yourself."

Now listen to the escalation of the denial.

The people in the courtyard say to Peter first of all, "You too were with Jesus." He responds, "I don't know him," and he separates himself from Jesus. Another person says to him, "Yes, you too were with his disciples." And he replies, "What you say is not true." Another one says, "You too were one of them and belonged to that group." "No, not me!" At the moment in which Peter breaks away from Jesus, he also loses his connection to the community of Jesus, to the Church. And finally, when he is told, "You were also with him, you yourself are a Galilean too" (he is recognized as a Galilean by his accent, his dialogue, and his clothes), Peter responds, "Hey, man! I don't know what you are talking about." Not only has he separated himself from Jesus, and in doing so lost connection with the disciples, but he also, being cut off from Jesus, loses awareness of his identity and no longer knows who he is.

This is the real tragedy of our betrayals and denials of Jesus. The moment in which we lose connection with Jesus and with the Church, we are no longer ourselves and we do not have any understanding of who we will be. For Peter at that moment, the cock crows and his crowing becomes an echo of Jesus's words during the Last Supper. Peter, now smitten and dejected, is brought back to self-awareness. The detailed coordinates have been verified; he is aware that what Jesus said to him at the Last Supper was precisely a prophecy.

The Lord, turning his head, looks at Peter. Once more it is the gaze of Jesus that conquers a person, that moves him to compassion. We can understand that this gaze is not the unpleasant gaze of "I told you so!" It is not a gaze of judgment but a gentle, tender gaze that seeks to win him back.

Jesus's gaze is a bit like his voice in Gethsemane when he calls Judas "Friend." It is a gaze that calls Peter back, but, unlike Judas, what does Peter do? He recalls the words the Lord had spoken, and he goes out weeping bitterly. These tears of suffering, of repentance for his denial, are a blessing for Peter because they are the prerequisite to receiving forgiveness. Judas betrayed Jesus, and when he realized he had spilled innocent blood, he despaired. He thought there was no possibility for salvation, so he killed himself. Peter, instead, goes out weeping and these tears are his request to Jesus to forgive him and to accept him again as a friend. The falling tears from this "Sandman, Sandman" mix with the dirt, and, not far from here in the Cenacle on the morning of Pentecost, that dirt mixed with the tears of suffering and repentance will be hardened into stone, as in a kiln, by the fire of the Holy Spirit. Then Simon will definitively become Peter, a solid rock on which finally the whole Church can remain firm; he knows he will never again deny his Lord. He might be weak, a sinner in his flesh, but he will not ever again betray Jesus; his faith will be sure, solid, and secure.

We can ask Peter's intercession here, on the one hand, never to deny Jesus, never to leave him, and, on the other hand, never to abandon the Church.

Do you remember Zacchaeus? He was short and could not see Jesus because of the crowd. So what did he do? He climbed a sycamore tree. What could the sycamore for us be that overcomes our spiritual weakness and allows us to go beyond all the obstacles that come our way from the outside? It is precisely the Church. If we climb the sycamore-Church, we will not become prone to opinions and wickedness because in the Church we are guaranteed the certainty of seeing Jesus.

Through Peter's intercession, let us ask to be able to remain with the Church and to have a clear consciousness of our identity at all times, not based on what we think of ourselves or on what others say about us—because that is almost always misleading—but based on our relationship with Jesus. Our self-understanding needs to start with our relationship with Jesus: I am a disciple of the Lord, of the Lord who decided to die and make himself a gift of love for me, of a Lord who is risen and alive.

Personal Reflection

I watch Jesus as he shepherds Peter. And I see Peter as he goes astray in denying Jesus and finds himself again, instructed in the truth and healed by repentance and forgiveness. And I ask myself:

1. Am I ever ashamed of Jesus, the Gospel, or the Church?
2. Do I rely on my enthusiasm and my efforts?
3. Do I let Jesus unmask my inconsistencies and weaknesses?
4. How do I live out my membership in the Church?
5. Do I know how to foster sincere repentance that leads me back to the demanding but liberating gaze of Jesus?

Prayer

O Lord Jesus, you safeguard us
through your prayer,
through your word of truth,
through the companionship of the Church.

O Lord Jesus, you free us
from our presumption,
from our deception,
from our despair.

O Lord Jesus, you alone are worthy
of all our praise,
of all our worship,
of all our allegiance.

16
·······
THE HOLY SEPULCHRE
The Resurrection

From the Gospel according to John (20:1-18)

Early on the first day of the week, while it was still dark, Mary Magdalene came to the tomb and saw that the stone had been removed from the tomb. So she ran and went to Simon Peter and the other disciple, the one whom Jesus loved, and said to them, "They have taken the Lord out of the tomb, and we do not know where they have laid him."

Then Peter and the other disciple set out and went toward the tomb. The two were running together, but the other disciple outran Peter and reached the tomb first. He bent down to look in and saw the linen wrappings lying there, but he did not go in. Then Simon Peter came, following him, and went into the tomb. He saw the linen wrappings lying there, and the cloth that had been on Jesus' head, not lying with the linen wrappings but rolled up in a place by itself. Then the other disciple, who reached the tomb first, also went in, and he saw and believed; for as yet they did not understand the scripture, that he must rise from the dead. Then the disciples returned to their homes.

But Mary stood weeping outside the tomb. As she wept, she bent over to look into the tomb; and she saw two angels in white, sitting where the body of Jesus had been lying, one at the head and the other at the feet. They said to her, "Woman, why are you weeping?" She said to them, "They have taken away my Lord, and I do not know where they have laid him." When she had said this, she turned around and saw Jesus standing there, but she did not know that it was Jesus. Jesus said to her, "Woman, why are you weeping? Whom are you looking for?" Supposing him to be the gardener, she said to him, "Sir, if you have carried him away, tell me where you have laid him, and I will take him away." Jesus said to her, "Mary!" She turned and said to him in

Hebrew, "Rabbouni!" (which means Teacher). Jesus said to her, "Do not hold on to me, because I have not yet ascended to the Father. But go to my brothers and say to them, 'I am ascending to my Father and your Father, to my God and your God.'" Mary Magdalene went and announced to the disciples, "I have seen the Lord"; and she told them that he had said these things to her.

MEDITATION

"Scimus Christum surrexisse a mortuis vere!" ("We know Christ is truly risen from the dead!")

In the wonderful sequence *"Victimae Paschali"* on Easter Sunday that precedes the Gospel, there is an extraordinary affirmation that can be paraphrased this way: "Yes, we know, and we know with deep delight, that this involves all of our lives, our faith, and our love; we know that Christ is truly risen."

In the great liturgical tradition of the Church, we are not content to say merely that Jesus is risen. We want to affirm that Jesus is risen and alive!

He did not simply come back to life so that he could die again. He was not brought back to life like Lazarus, whom Jesus rescued from the tomb and would then have to die again. Jesus is risen and alive: He will no longer ever die. If Jesus is alive it means that he is our contemporary; we can dialogue with him and perceive his attentive and loving gaze on our lives; we can look at him and recognize in him the reality of our own lives.

To know that Jesus is risen and alive means that he has truly defeated the power of death. He has rescued us from the mortal anguish that comes from the mystery of death that manifests itself as a kind of declaration of bankruptcy about life. The big problem with death is not only that it puts an end to life, but it also echoes that our existence is a kind of failure: All that we do or suffer or work at and all we have loved, experienced, or endured has been useless and seems to affirm death.

The resurrection, life that is no longer subject to death, gives a fullness of meaning and beauty to the day-to-day nature of our existence; every effort, hope, suffering, and desire finds its true significance.

Here in the Basilica of the Holy Sepulchre—because of St Helena's efforts and the assistance of bishops who encouraged the construction of this church—the whole paschal mystery of the passion, death, and resurrection is brought together. Here, in fact, we find Golgotha (Calvary), where Jesus was lifted up on the cross and the sepulchre in which he was buried and from which he emerged victorious. It is here that Jesus endured the final hours of his earthly life and gave himself over definitively to the Father. It is here that he was buried and then showed himself to be alive after the women and the disciples found the empty tomb.

Let us listen again, especially through John's narrative, to some of the events on Easter morning and the attitude of the disciples who rushed there.

After the women told the disciples they had found the tomb empty, Peter and John rush to the tomb—an absorbing and intense race.

They run there at the first light of dawn. They leave the Cenacle, which is not far away, as the crow flies, indifferent to all the dangers they could encounter. John, the youngest, Jesus's friend with a contemplative nature, runs the most vigorously and arrives first, but he stops at the threshold. He is almost afraid of violating the mystery before him and waits for Peter to enter first because he was made the head of the apostolic college. Peter has to confirm his own faith so that he can, in turn, confirm the faith of the brothers and sisters. When Peter, who is older and perhaps more tired, reaches the tomb, he rushes in with the enthusiasm that has always characterized him.

When John enters next into the innermost room of the tomb, he notices some specific details. He sees that things are very orderly: There are no traces of a moving of the body or of a violent or hasty theft. There are no signs of torn wrapping cloths or burglary. There is order and peace here: The linen cloths were not in disarray, and even the napkin that covered his face was folded and carefully laid out. The commentary is striking: "He saw and believed."

John's contemplative gaze succeeds in grasping, behind the signs he sees, the mystery that has been fulfilled. All of the Fourth Gospel is filled with the verbs *come* and *see*. Merely being with Jesus and sharing his life, John had learned to see with the eyes of faith. "Come" and "see" now become "believe."

In entering the sepulchre today, we too want to apprehend the fact of it being empty. We invested our energy and followed our desire to arrive here to find an empty tomb. The empty tomb is decisive for our faith: It confirms to us that Jesus is risen and alive.

We encounter him in the liturgical reading of the Gospel and in the celebration of the Eucharist, in the body he gave and the blood he poured out. In this sacrifice that is renewed every time we celebrate Mass, we encounter the Lord and are reached by him and his grace. We are *touched by Jesus*, and his touch saves us.

Here in this garden, Magdalene is also met by Jesus. Let us recall the Gospel episode recounting that Mary Magdalene is outside the tomb and is weeping because Jesus's body is not there anymore. She is weeping because even this man's body has been taken away from her—this man who came into her life and set her free from evil, regenerating her and giving her life meaning and beauty. She had been at the foot of the cross and was able to see her Lord giving himself completely out of love, and she is here now and continues to grieve. Her impassioned search and weeping make her able to be encountered by Jesus who calls out her name: "Mary!" He calls her by name; he calls her to a new relationship. When he met her for the first time and had found her enslaved to her sin, he called her and brought her to the new dignity of being a free woman, a restored woman, and had introduced her to a friendship with himself. Now he calls her again, but this time to a new life of friendship with the Risen One. Like the spouse in the Song of Songs, Mary is rewarded for her passionate search. Just as the woman in the Song of Songs had experienced the love and the loving embrace of her spouse, Mary had had the opportunity to experience the goodness of communion with Jesus. Suddenly deprived of her spouse's presence in the Song of Songs, the bride went out into the night to search for him. Magdalene is also outside the tomb and is in search of Jesus, in a night of solitude, anguish, and desperation. Finally the bride in the Song of Songs encounters her spouse and exclaims, "I found my heart's beloved; I embrace him and will never again leave him!" Magdalene seeks to embrace Jesus, to hold him to herself and not ever lose him. However, Jesus stops her, saying, "I must ascend to my Father." He is not removing himself from her but is giving himself in a new way. He commissions Mary Magdalene to bring to his disciples the Easter announcement that now there is no more separation, no more time of fasting, suffering, and struggle because it is wedding time, the wedding of Christ and his Church.

In this holy place, let us allow ourselves to be led to faith. Let us ask for the grace to discover Jesus risen and alive. We, too, decide to embrace him and let ourselves be embraced. The definitive and eternal wedding between the Lord Jesus and our souls, between the Lord Jesus and our lives, is truly fulfilled in the Eucharist. All of our daily existence becomes transformed and transfigured by his presence.

Personal Reflection

I fix my gaze on the empty tomb. I contemplate that emptiness, and I ask myself:

1. Do I really believe in Jesus's resurrection? Do I know with the certainty of faith that Jesus is risen and alive?

2. Knowing that he is alive, do I relate to Jesus as my contemporary? Or do I have a kind of vague esteem for him as people do for a historical figure in the past?

3. Is my spiritual life characterized by a passionate search for the Lord's presence?

4. Do I joyfully announce to brothers and sisters that Jesus is risen and alive?

5. Do I recognize the presence of the Risen One in the life of the Church: in its liturgy, in its proclamation of the word of God, and in its sacraments?

6. Jesus is risen and alive. How does this fundamental truth concretely affect my Christian life?

PRAYER

I *believe* in you, Lord, risen and alive.
Help my unbelief.

I *hope* in you, Lord, for life and resurrection.
Sustain my hope.

I *love* you, Lord, your grace and mercy.
Rekindle my seeking of your presence.

17
. . . .

TABGHA
The Primacy of Peter

From the Gospel according to John (21:1-19)

After these things Jesus showed himself again to the disciples by the Sea of Tiberias; and he showed himself in this way. Gathered there together were Simon Peter, Thomas called the Twin, Nathanael of Cana in Galilee, the sons of Zebedee, and two others of his disciples. Simon Peter said to them, "I am going fishing." They said to him, "We will go with you." They went out and got into the boat, but that night they caught nothing.

Just after daybreak, Jesus stood on the beach; but the disciples did not know that it was Jesus. Jesus said to them, "Children, you have no fish, have you?" They answered him, "No." He said to them, "Cast the net to the right side of the boat, and you will find some." So they cast it, and now they were not able to haul it in because there were so many fish. That disciple whom Jesus loved said to Peter, "It is the Lord!" When Simon Peter heard that it was the Lord, he put on some clothes, for he was naked, and jumped into the sea. But the other disciples came in the boat, dragging the net full of fish, for they were not far from the land, only about a hundred yards off.

When they had gone ashore, they saw a charcoal fire there, with fish on it, and bread. Jesus said to them, "Bring some of the fish that you have just caught." So Simon Peter went aboard and hauled the net ashore, full of large fish, a hundred fifty-three of them; and though there were so many, the net was not torn. Jesus said to them, "Come and have breakfast." Now none of the disciples dared to ask him, "Who are you?" because they knew it was the Lord. Jesus came and took the bread and gave it to them, and did the same with the fish. This was now the third time that Jesus appeared to the disciples after he was raised from the dead.

When they had finished breakfast, Jesus said to Simon Peter,

"Simon son of John, do you love me more than these?" He said to him, "Yes, Lord; you know that I love you." Jesus said to him, "Feed my lambs." A second time he said to him, "Simon son of John, do you love me?" He said to him, "Yes, Lord; you know that I love you." Jesus said to him, "Tend my sheep." He said to him the third time, "Simon son of John, do you love me?" Peter felt hurt because he said to him the third time, "Do you love me?" And he said to him, "Lord, you know everything; you know that I love you." Jesus said to him, "Feed my sheep. Very truly, I tell you, when you were younger, you used to fasten your own belt and to go wherever you wished. But when you grow old, you will stretch out your hands, and someone else will fasten a belt around you and take you where you do not wish to go." (He said this to indicate the kind of death by which he would glorify God.) After this he said to him, "Follow me."

MEDITATION

We read in chapter twenty-one of John's Gospel, "After these things Jesus showed himself again to the disciples." After what things? After the events surrounding Easter. The resurrection has already occurred and a group of seven disciples, all from this area, are in this place. Why were they here? Why weren't they in Jerusalem? We can list two reasons. The first is that they perhaps did not really know what to do, so they returned home where they felt more comfortable in familiar surroundings. But they had also returned home in obedience to the directive Jesus had given them through the women: "Tell my brothers to go to Galilee; there they will see me" (Matthew 28:10). But why Galilee in particular? Because that is where it all started. It was on the shore of this lake that Jesus had called his first disciples; they had been with him and learned, saw, and heard from him right up to his death and resurrection. They often understood nothing and were disoriented. However, now that Jesus had risen, it was possible to understand everything. It is as if Jesus were saying, "Go back to the beginning; go back to the beginning now with the light of Easter, and in that light you will understand everything that has happened. Now the plan has been completed and you can understand it." Easter thus becomes the interpretive key to everything. Why in Galilee? Because Galilee is the place of everyday life. We can have many intense experiences of the Lord, but the proof that our communion with him is authentic—that we have understood who is for our lives—occurs in our ordinary lives. During extraordinary experiences this is essentially easy for everyone, but it is in the test of daily life that we have to see if we are authentic disciples of the Lord.

Peter and the others are here. Peter says, "Well, while I am waiting, there is one thing I know how to do. I know this lake, so I am going fishing." He takes the initiative and the others respond, "We will go with you too." They do not know if Peter is doing the right thing, but that is what Peter is doing. They have understood by now that they must go where Peter goes because it is his job to guide them. This time Peter actually makes a kind of mistake in the sense that he decides this by himself and not in obedience to Jesus. He takes the initiative, but it is still a human initiative. He does what he feels like doing and what comes naturally and spontaneously. As a matter of fact, they go out on one of the most fished lakes on earth. They work using all the techniques that Peter remembers well. He had many years of experience, but they did not catch anything. Something was not working right: They did not go in obedience but on their own initiative. Jesus appears. The risen Jesus makes himself be seen, and at first they do not recognize him. He asks, "Didn't you catch anything?" "Nothing, Lord, and we worked all night but…" Jesus tells them, "Cast the net to the right side of the boat," and this time, as they obeyed, they caught a superabundant quantity of fish. Notice that after they caught the fish, John, the contemplative one, finally recognizes Jesus and says to the others, "It is the Lord!" Peter is aware of his wretchedness, of his poverty; he is naked so he clothes himself because, before the mystery of God, one needs to have an attitude of holiness and reverential fear. The disciples reach Jesus and he asks them, "Bring me the fish that you have just caught." They drag their net full of 153 large fish unto the shore. However, they eat other fish, the fish that Jesus had cooked on his charcoal fire, so they did not eat the fish they had caught.

There are a series of details here worth noting and analyzing. Jesus facilitates this miraculous catch not so much to demonstrate his power but because he was giving a task to his Church, to Peter, and the others. In biblical symbolism, great bodies of water are a sign of sin and death. For a semi-nomadic people who live in the desert (like the Jews when they lived in Egypt), having to face a great body of water presents an enormous uncertainty. How did freedom from slavery in Egypt happen? By the people passing over to dry land in the midst of the water of the Red Sea and overcoming its danger. Great bodies of water are such a sign of sin and death that Revelation tells us there will be a new heaven and a new earth, but *"the sea was no more"* (21:1); in Revelation there is resurrection, so death and sin are no more. What does Jesus make his disciples do? He makes them cast their net; he does not make them fish with hooks that kill the fish but with a net that pulls the fish up out of the water. If water is a sign of sin and death, it means that he is commanding them to rescue something from the power of sin and death in order to give it life, and then he asks them, "Bring them here to me." He is the Risen One who has definitively conquered. So we begin to suspect that these fish are not simply fish that live in the water but are symbols of something else, symbols of humanity. This is why the Gospel writer tells us there are 153 fish. It is not that he merely felt like counting them to rejoice at the great catch. No, it was because 153 is the number of known species of fish in the Lake of Tiberias. This says it all in a nutshell: Through this particular fishing experience, Jesus wanted to direct his Church to universal evangelization. "My word is like a large net thrown into the sea of humanity that is immersed in sin and death. Catch the people and bring them to me. Freed from sin and death, they can enter into friendship with me, and that will bring them to salvation." Therefore, Peter and those with him, who were accustomed to being fishermen and catching live fish and then killing them to eat them, at this point will begin to do the exact opposite. They will snatch them from death and lead them to life. This is why the Synoptic Gospels say, "You will no longer catch fish but be fishers of people." In John's Gospel this saying is not found at the beginning but is placed at the end, after the resurrection.

After this comes the wonderful dialogue between Jesus and Peter. "Simon son of John,"—Jesus calls him by his old name, his human name and not the prestigious name connected to his ministry—"do you love me more than these?" Peter replies, "Lord, you know that I love you." There are three Greek verbs to say "I love": *erotao, fileo, agapao*. *Erotao* is not used in this passage. *Fileo* is the expression for friendship love and *agapao* is the expression for the love that is typical of God, charity, that is, love that makes a gift of its life. Jesus is asking him, "Do you love me with agape love, the love that I demonstrated on the cross some days ago, the love that makes you come out of yourself to become a gift for others?" And Peter, who is no longer the man he was earlier—the one who used to say, "I will come with you; I will do the job; I will teach you what you should do and say"—has now undergone the humiliation that springs from the awareness of his weakness, so he responds this way: "Look, Jesus, I love you, but *fileo*; I know I love you only with friendship love." "Well, then," Jesus says, "feed my lambs." For the second time, Jesus asks him, "Simon, do you love me with the agape love I showed you on the cross?" "Look, Lord, I honestly do love you with friendship love, *fileo*; that is what I have, and I give it all to you, but I do not have agape love yet." Jesus responds, "Then tend my sheep." Jesus asks again the third time, "Simon, you love me with friendship love; we know that you are at least giving me that love. Do you guarantee me that love?" Peter remains sorrowful and as if to say, "Yes, Jesus, I need to be content with that." Jesus starts with what Peter is capable of giving. Peter says, "Yes, Jesus, I can guarantee you *fileo*; I can give you friendship love." Jesus responds, "Feed my sheep. However, I have one thing to say to you. I will take you from here, from the friendship love you are capable of giving me. However, do not stop there; I will carry you further on. As a young man, you alone clothed yourself and went wherever you wanted. But when you are older someone else will clothe you and take you where you do not want to do go. Know that you too will live out the same gift of love that I did on the cross and will imitate me in martyrdom. It is true that you love me only with friendship love now, but you will become capable of divine love. Follow me." Jesus ends all this by telling him, "Follow me."

PERSONAL REFLECTION

I look at Peter and the other disciples and I ask myself:

1. How do I live out my membership in the Church?
2. What kind of obedience characterizes my relationship to the Successor of Peter?
3. How do I face daily life? Does the light of Easter illuminate my understanding of reality?
4. Are my choices simply the results of my own planning, or do they represent obedience to the Lord who manifests himself in his word and through discernment?
5. Do I feel a desire to proclaim to everyone the Gospel that rescues people from sin and death?

6. Am I humble in my relationship with Jesus? Am I aware of my weakness and of his love?

7. Do I allow Jesus to increase my love?

PRAYER

O Lord, you gave yourself without reserve;
you desire to draw all human beings to yourself;
you do not tire of enveloping us with your love.

O Lord, you sent the apostles
to spread your kingdom.
Build up the Church in truth and love,
and let not the gifts of grace for salvation be lacking.

O Lord, you take care of your disciples;
you love everyone in a personal way;
you wait for all the love that everyone is capable of.

O Lord, take me as I am.
Free me from sin that holds me captive,
And make me grow in your likeness.

18
. . . .

EMMAUS
Risen and with Us Always

From the Gospel according to Luke 24:13-35

Now on that same day two of them were going to a village called Emmaus, about seven miles from Jerusalem, and talking with each other about all these things that had happened. While they were talking and discussing, Jesus himself came near and went with them, but their eyes were kept from recognizing him. And he said to them, "What are you discussing with each other while you walk along?" They stood still, looking sad. Then one of them, whose name was Cleopas, answered him, "Are you the only stranger in Jerusalem who does not know the things that have taken place there in these days?" He asked them, "What things?" They replied, "The things about Jesus of Nazareth, who was a prophet mighty in deed and word before God and all the people, and how our chief priests and leaders handed him over to be condemned to death and crucified him. But we had hoped that he was the one to redeem Israel. Yes, and besides all this, it is now the third day since these things took place. Moreover, some women of our group astounded us. They were at the tomb early this morning, and when they did not find his body there, they came back and told us that they had indeed seen a vision of angels who said that he was alive. Some of those who were with us went to the tomb and found it just as the women had said; but they did not see him." Then he said to them, "Oh, how foolish you are, and how slow of heart to believe all that the prophets have declared! Was it not necessary that the Messiah should suffer these things and then enter into his glory?" Then beginning with Moses and all the prophets, he interpreted to them the things about himself in all the scriptures.

As they came near the village to which they were going, he walked ahead as if he were going on. But they urged him strongly, saying, "Stay with us, because it is almost evening and the day is now nearly over." So he went in to stay with them. When he was at the table with them, he took bread, blessed and broke it, and gave it to them. Then their eyes were opened, and they recognized him; and he vanished from their sight. They said to each other, "Were not our hearts burning within us while he was talking to us on the road, while he was opening the scriptures to us?" That same hour they got up and returned to Jerusalem; and they found the eleven and their companions gathered together. They were saying, "The Lord has risen indeed, and he has appeared to Simon!" Then they told what had happened on the road, and how he had been made known to them in the breaking of the bread.

MEDITATION

This is an extraordinary passage.

It is the first day after the Sabbath. It is Easter Sunday, the day that began at the first light of dawn that now never ends. Luke 24 completes the itinerary from Galilee to Jerusalem on which his Gospel is structured.

Luke's account begins with the Annunciation, with the beginning of a new day that will gradually expand and encompass all of history and all of humanity right up to this point.

Jesus included his disciples in this itinerary. He gradually tried to adjust their mindset and direct them toward Jerusalem.

Luke 9:51 includes a remarkable statement: "He set his face to go to Jerusalem." Jesus made a firm decision: Jerusalem was the place he had to go, the place of God's presence, the place of obedience to the Father, and the place of his supreme sacrifice. There, the days and events of the Passover, the passion, death, and resurrection would unfold. After these events one fundamental question arises for these first disciples: After this absolutely unheard of event, how were they supposed to live? Their issue was understanding what to do next.

The Gospel says that two disciples from Emmaus will not immediately penetrate the truth of this mystery and will choose exactly the opposite path by distancing themselves from Jerusalem. They had earlier been headed straight to Jerusalem where Jesus had led them, involving them in his life and fascinating them.

Leaving Jerusalem after so much hardship is a dramatic choice. They are returning to their village with who knows what turmoil in their hearts. Apart from the tremendous pain of having their dream shattered, they also had the stress of returning home where everyone would probably mock them. "Look at these guys who took off. They left everything; they abandoned their work and their life goals to follow this prophet, and look how he ended up: He died on a cross. Now they have to return and come back here disheartened." From the emotional and psychological point of view, these are not simple steps they have to go through.

Jesus does not give up in the face of the hardness of heart of the disciples, so he comes alongside them on their journey. He listens to their dialogue and knows they are talking about all that had happened, going back over all the events of recent days. Jesus approaches them with great sensitivity. He wants to understand what is truly in their hearts, but above all he wants them to become aware of their mistaken understanding of those events. He actually approaches them almost as though he is a stranger. Why were the disciples incapable of recognizing him? The reasons could be quite trivial. When people are walking down a road, they shield their faces from the sunlight and the dust on the road, so Jesus was not very visible. This reason, though, is not sufficient because if people looked into Jesus's eyes they would certainly recognize him. The issue is a different one: These two disciples were unduly focused on themselves. They were aware that another traveler had joined them, but probably neither of them even looked at him. They were so concentrated on themselves and their troubles that they did not even look at Jesus.

This also says a lot about our spiritual life. At times we are so focused on ourselves that even if the Lord is there alongside us to reach us where we are and to rescue us, we do not see him. We perhaps might even complain, "Lord, where are you? Why have you abandoned me?" But he is there.

Jesus asks them a question: "What are you discussing with each other while you walk along?" He is prodding them; he wants them to narrate the events of those days. He pretends not to know what happened, and this shocks them: "Did you really just leave the same city we did? Jerusalem is not that big, and people everywhere are talking only about the events surrounding Jesus of Nazareth. How can you not know these things?" Jesus's question about what they are discussing with each other could be paralleled, from a certain point of view, by the following image: "What are these heavy burdens that you are declaring to each other and heaping on each other?"

These two disciples are accurately narrating the episodes of Jesus's life. They had lived through them with him. They are recounting what Jesus did, and during their report they probably became passionate and enthusiastic like people who recount a wonderful event and put their soul into it. The conclusion, however, is chilling: "We had hoped he was the one, but he died and people say that even his body is gone. They expect us to believe he is risen, but we have no evidence to believe a thing like that."

Let us try to see the pattern in their telling of the story. Going back over all the stages of their friendship with Jesus reawakens their sentiments, their joy, the goodness of belonging to Jesus. It makes them appreciate again all the decisions they made, their courageous choice to leave everything to be with him. However, things ended tragically with Jesus's death on the cross. This has the destructive force of a "heavy burden" that crushes all their joy and enthusiasm. We also need to experience the same pattern: Let us reassess events and be enthusiastic as we think about the past; however, since we, too, have our own interpretive thought patterns, let us put those to death with "we had hoped...but it is all over now."

This dreadful attitude makes them unable to recognize him. They have their rigid interpretation and are not open to the news that reaches them and surprises them.

After listening to their narration and making them bring back to mind the wonderful things they had experienced, Jesus helps them to become aware of the mistaken dynamic of their attitude toward reality. "Oh, how foolish and slow of heart you are to understand the scriptures and the prophets. Was not the Christ supposed to endure all these things?" It is as if Jesus were saying, "You continue to apply an interpretive approach to the Messiah that prevents you from recognizing him as risen because you were scandalized by the cross. If you listen to Scripture, it is precisely Scripture that says things had to be this way, that what happened in Jerusalem is not a scandal but truth." Then Jesus begins to call to their minds all the passages in the Old Testament that are essential to understanding the Lord's cross in a different way. Let us try to imagine the scene of the disciples who are walking with Jesus at their side for about seven miles as he speaks about the Old Testament and interprets it, revealing the exact significance of prophecies and events. We can almost picture them in our minds: Initially focused on themselves with downcast faces, little by little they regain their strength, lift up their heads, return to an upright position, and breathe deeply again. Having reached the village of Emmaus, Jesus concretely checks to see if these two have understood and accepted all that he wanted to reveal to them during their journey. The Gospel account states, "He walked ahead as if he were going on."

But they urge him, "Stay with us, because it is almost evening and the day is now nearly over." The disciples' invitation shows that they accepted the extraordinary nature of their mysterious journey companion. This could, of course, seem like a simple gesture of hospitality, since it could in fact have been dangerous to be out in the streets at night. However, their invitation reveals the new feeling that is now in the hearts of these two. "It would be very good if you stayed with us. We have not yet understood who you are, but your presence is a source of consolation. Stay here with us."

They enter the place, and during the meal Jesus performs actions and repeats the very words of consecration for the Eucharist. He takes the bread and breaks it. (In the first centuries of the Church the Mass was called *Fractio Panis,* "The Breaking of the Bread.") The disciples—watching this take place and trained in listening to the word of God now being interpreted by the great exegete who had joined them—are able to recognize him in the breaking of the bread.

The Gospel reports that at the disciples' invitation, Jesus "went in to stay with them." As soon as they recognized him, however, "he vanished from their sight." But why? Shouldn't he have stayed with them? Why did he vanish from their sight? Because now he was still with them, because he had taught them to recognize him in the sacrament of his presence that he had left them: the body broken for them and the blood poured out for them.

We find the same pattern in the structure of the Mass: the Liturgy of the Word leads us to the Liturgy of the Eucharist and allows us to recognize Jesus, risen and alive, and really present in the Eucharist.

Jesus disappears and the disciples say to one another, "Were not our hearts burning within us while he was opening the scriptures to us?" We, too, can have this experience: The word of God is a fire that revives our hearts and opens us up to hope again.

What did the two disciples do? Despite their weariness and the potential dangers, they run back to Jerusalem where the Christian community is living. When they arrive at the Cenacle, even before they can speak, the apostles themselves announce to them, "The Lord has risen indeed, and he has appeared to Simon!" It is crucial that Jesus appeared to Simon Peter because he is the one who confirms the others in their faith. The two from Emmaus have returned to Jerusalem, and their meeting with Peter and the community gathered in the Cenacle confirms their renewed faith in their encounter with the Risen One.

The nearly seven miles traveled by the disciples from Emmaus in Jesus's company can be an effective and concise image of our own journey. Jesus himself has explained Scripture to us a little at a time. He has made us relive the basic events of his life in the very places in which they occurred so that we could encounter him and recognize him—especially on Sunday in the Christian community—as present, risen, and alive in the celebration of the Eucharist.

We do not need anything else to face daily life with its difficulties because the only news we need to sustain our lives and to proclaim to others is that the Lord is risen and alive.

Personal Reflection

I see the journey of the two disciples who leave Jerusalem. I see their anguish and sadness. As I see Jesus come alongside them, I admire his sensitivity and resolve, and I ask myself:

1. Am I a prisoner of my thoughts and my interpretive approaches?
2. Where do my anxieties and disappointments come from?
3. What causes my heart to be hardened and my eyes to be blinded?
4. Do I cherish the memories of God's action in my life with gratitude and amazement?
5. Does listening to the word of God make my heart burn within me, rekindling my hope and healing my eyes so that I am able to recognize Jesus's real presence in the Eucharist and in the Church?

PRAYER

What sensitivity you have, Lord,
in coming alongside those who have lost heart!
What tenderness you have
in listening to our anguish!
What wisdom you have
in leading us to the truth!

Consider again, Lord,
our weakness.
Listen again
to our cry.
Free us again
from our prisons.

Stay with us, Lord,
and always shine your light on us.
Touch us with your grace,
and let our life be ever new.
Show yourself present and alive,
and let our joy always be authentic.

ABOUT THE AUTHOR

Vincenzo Peroni, priest of the Diocese of Brescia since 1994, has served pastorally in the parishes of Sarezzo and Manerbio and in various diocesan assignments. In 2012 he obtained a License in Spiritual Theology (at the Faculty of Theology at Triveneto). Since 2010 he has served at the Holy See in the Office for Pontifical Liturgical Celebrations and as a Papal Master of Ceremonies since 2012. He has led numerous pilgrimages in the Holy Land.